ballroom dancing

paul bottomer

A CONNECTIONS • AXIS EDITION

A Connections • Axis Edition

This edition first published in Great Britain by
Connections Book Publishing Limited
St Chad's House
148 King's Cross Road
London WC1X 9DH
and Axis Publishing Limited
8c Accommodation Road
London NW11 8ED
www.axispublishing.co.uk

Conceived and created by
Axis Publishing Limited

Creative Director: Siân Keogh
Managing Editor: Brian Burns
Project Designer: Sean Keogh
Project Editor: Antony Atha
Photographer: Mike Good

Note
The opinions and advice expressed in this book are intended as a guide only. The publisher and author accept no responsibility for any injury or loss sustained as a result of using this book.

British Library Cataloguing-in-Publication data available on request.

ISBN 1–85906–094–3

9 8 7 6 5 4 3 2

Separation by United Graphics Pte Limited
Printed and bound by Star Standard (Pte) Limited

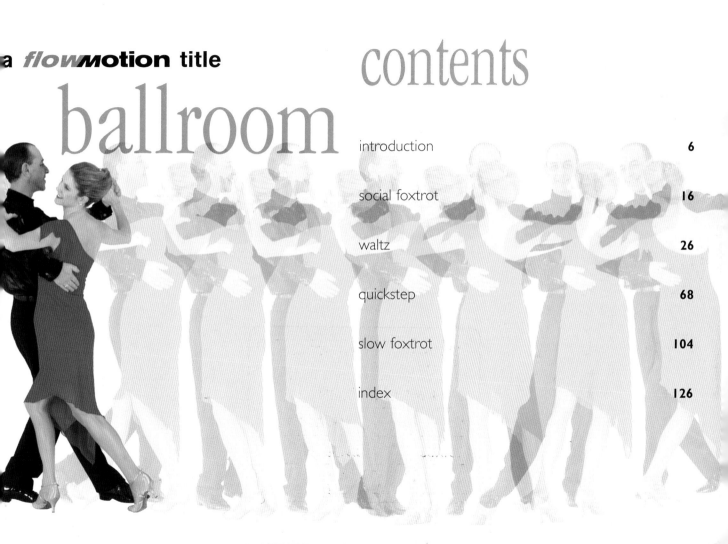

a ***flowmotion*** title

ballroom

contents

introduction

If, as is often said, language reveals the mind, then the language of dance reveals the soul. This simple yet profound truth has been a feature of human life ever since our ancestors first felt emotions. Since prehistory, the human soul has been stirred into movement as a natural, instinctive and sometimes even primordial response to the sounds of the natural world; sounds that when ordered and repeated became the first rhythms. These rhythms of nature inevitably evoked a physical response, and our ancestors took their first steps towards dancing. Later, as the human brain evolved, our forebears became skilled and adept at actively generating more sophisticated rhythms and sounds, without being restricted to naturally occurring percussion. This became the music of the world. As the human race evolved, music also became more sophisticated, reflecting moods, emotions and the world in which our ancestors lived. With sharper minds and fitter bodies, over time the music that people made became more expressive, heightening the emotions and prompting the physical response we know as dancing. Dancing became one way that we define our humanity, our view of the world, how we project ourselves, anc how we give expression to our innermos feelings, our nature and our soul.

Today, there is a bewildering variety o dance forms. These dances are all shaped by thei particular geographical, social and cultura environments. Dancing can define the prevailin mood of an era and, sometimes, it can even come tc symbolise the aspirations a generation. Music anc dance, of course, also evoke memories of time and place Now, thanks to modern communications, all types of musi can easily be downloaded, anywhere in the world, at the click of a mouse. New technology also allows us to listen tc music just about anywhere – in the car, on the train, in the office, and even walking down the street

Musical styles, and their associated dances, have alsc crossed cultural borders. Ballroom dancing, for example, i now no longer merely a classic, popular style of partne dancing, it is also the recognized style of partner dancing, witl

The enjoyment of the dance is very evident when a couple move in complete harmony

internationally agreed standards, for historical provenance, format, structure and performance style.

For some people, dance is a great opportunity to get away from their normal, everyday world and escape to another, more diverting, place. It is an easily accessed, highly convenient and very inexpensive 'holiday' for a few hours, away from the demands of the frenetic, modern world. For others, it is a chance to meet like-minded people who share their passion for music and dance, and have come to soak up the atmosphere. It is no accident that dancing is inextricably bound up with life's happier moments.

The image of the dance is portrayed in the flowing images of the couple around the floor

waltz

Some people waltz in the hope of starting a new relationship during the evening's last dance. Newly-weds play a Waltz at their wedding reception to break down barriers and create a warm, relaxed mood. Wherever it is played, the Waltz is the only dance with innate and timeless romance, the source of its enduring appeal. But the Waltz also evolves and adapts to suit the dominant musical style of the day. For example, the romance of the Waltz is currently complemented by some of the best modern ballads and soft rock classics. Many young people have discovered that they too can enjoy applying these classic dances to contemporary chart music. Not only is classic Ballroom dancing preparing for inclusion in the Olympic games (possibly in 2008), it is also thriving among students at many of the world's universities, both at straightforward social events and at competitive levels.

The romance of the Waltz is always linked with the music of Strauss and Franz Lehár's *Merry Widow*

a scandalous history

Characterised by its gyratory movements, the Waltz started life as an Austrian folk-dance called the 'Ländler'. Although the origins of the Waltz may be charmingly rustic and innocuous, by the beginning of the 19th century, it had become socially controversial. A new hold was taken up in which the man would place his hand around the woman's body, which was, according to the social codes of the time, considered by many people as scandalous and unseemly. The public furore that followed was only resolved when Tsar Alexander of Russia gave the dance his royal seal of approval by performing the Waltz openly and in public. By the end of the 19th century, the fabulous music of the Strauss family, Franz Lehár and others had transformed the Waltz into the most romantic and glamorous of dances.

a new mood

As the 20th century began, a new mood took hold: the world became less formal and more relaxed. A new dance called the Boston, though not itself destined to last, brought about another change in the Waltz. In a less stylized and formal hold, the dancers moved closer together and made contact at the hips and lower abdomen. The pace of the Waltz also became more relaxed and leisurely: the tempo of the modern Waltz has slowed to half that of the original Viennese Waltz.

Views of upper body shaping enhanced in flowmotion

foxtrot

While the modern Waltz has its own special rhythm, expressing its 3/4 time signature, most enduring popular music has been composed, written and arranged with a standard 4/4 time signature. Most popular dances, therefore, work within this musical framework. The Foxtrot and the faster Quickstep are examples of the most popular of these dances.

Mr Fox

The Foxtrot emerged in the early 20th century at around the time of World War I. An American comedian called Harry Fox performed his act in the burlesque theatres of the day. The law permitted semi-clad females to appear on stage in these venues in 'artistic' poses, but it did not allow them to move or act in a way that could be considered 'indecorous' according to the social conventions of the period. Harry Fox probably felt upstaged as he vied for the audience's attention, plying his act amid the scantily clad models. Therefore, as part of his routine, he devised a comical dance movement as he moved around the stage from one model to the next to deliver his jokes. This 'dance' became the signature of his now-famous act. The popular music industry, known then as 'Tin-Pan Alley', hit on the idea of marketing music so that the general public could enjoy dancing their own versions of Harry Fox's 'Trot' or – as it became known – the 'Fox-Trot'. This new daring dance, with its suggestion of rebellious impropriety, was given added impetus by new moves created and choreographed by dance teachers. The dance halls were soon packed with people clamouring for the fashionable Foxtrot. As time went by, the dance developed from its humble background and risqué origins, to become more refined and sophisticated. By 1916, a new style of Foxtrot had emerged that was less brash. It now incorporated a slower, more elegant, gliding feel and went on to become one of the most popular dances of all time: the Slow Foxtrot. During the 1930s and 1940s, the golden age of Swing, the style of the music was reflected in the dance as it took on a graceful flow, using body swing, rise, and fall. The technique required to master the feeling of the dance became ever more demanding, but equally more rewarding. Most Ballroom dancers dream of excelling at the Slow Foxtrot.

Yet the original Foxtrot, with its vivacious character and the lively atmosphere it generated, was not forgotten. Rather, it was adapted to reflect the music of the moment – Jazz. During the 1920s, the original Foxtrot got jazzed up and was played ever faster. It was danced at a blistering pace as the Quick Time Foxtrot. By the mid-1920s, the Charleston had appeared as a new, fun dance craze. Although it made quite an impact, the Charleston's potential as a dance was limited. Its moves and its feel remained popular, however, and, when the fad ended, these aspects were adapted into the 'Quick Time Foxtrot and Charleston' – a cumbersome name that was soon shortened to 'Quickstep'. The Quickstep remains popular today, with its unique combination of the flowing, sweeping movements around the floor, interspersed with explosive highlights of syncopated jazzy hops and skips.

Each different dance has its own individual character. Now, through the innovative technique of Flowmotion, you can 'see' the feeling that the dancers experience, captured in space and time, as they create and develop the movement through a particular figure or dance sequence.

Dancing exists on many different levels: for social gatherings; for physical fitness and mental sharpness; as a means of personal expression; as a stress-busting escape; as a means of finding not just a dance partner, but a life partner; or simply as fun. Whatever the motivation, dancing is all to do with feeling that unique combination of movement to music.

The Foxtrot in full swing

the hold

The Ballroom hold described applies to all the dances in this book. It is the starting position to take up before a Ballroom dance begins. The man initiates the hold by taking the woman's right hand in his left hand and drawing her towards him. This immediately allows him to position her a little on his right-hand side. When this is done correctly, an imaginary central line through the man's body should be facing the woman's right shoulder.

In taking up the hold, the man presents his left hand, palm open and facing the woman as if he is making a 'stop' signal. The woman responds by placing the hooked middle finger of her right hand between the thumb and forefinger of the man's left hand, palm to palm. Next, the woman moves the forefinger and third finger of her right hand on top of her middle finger. Finally, she rests her little finger on top of the others and curls her thumb around the man's thumb. After the hands have been joined in this way, they should be held just below the couple's eye-level, with the handhold and arms kept firm but not rigid. At this point, the man positions the fingertips of his left hand along the edge of the woman's right hand, his fingers pointing to the floor. This manoeuvre leaves the underside of the man's left wrist and the woman's right wrist facing the floor. When a couple starts to dance, this position improves balance and makes it much easier for the man to lead.

The Ballroom hold is completed by the following procedure. The man cups the woman's left shoulder blade with his right hand, with the fingertips positioned against the woman's backbone. Meanwhile, the woman straightens the fingers of her left hand, and places her left hand on the man's upper arm with a straight and flat wrist. Both the man and the woman should hold their elbows slightly forward of the position occupied by their backs and away from their bodies. The shoulders should be relaxed; and never hunched up or tense.

The dynamic flow of the Quickstep

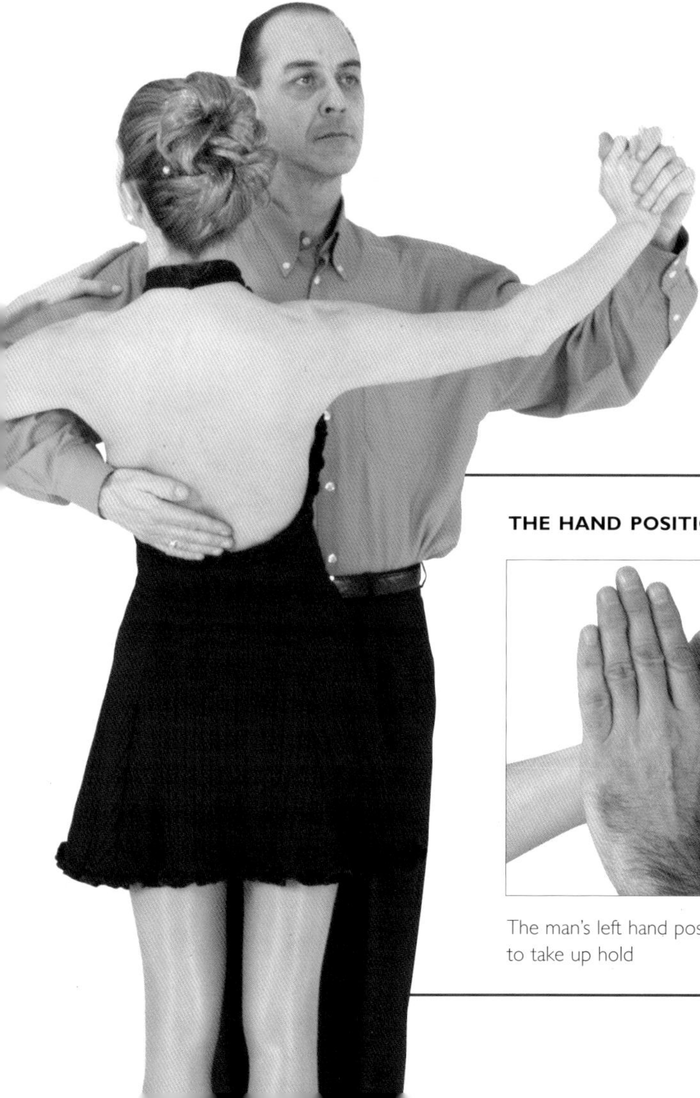

Finally, the man and the woman should both stand straight, lifting the diaphragm to produce a good posture. The couple should hold their heads slightly to the left, with the chin up, looking at the horizon not at the position of their feet. The heaviness of the head can make the hold unstable if the couple do not take up the desired position. In summary, the man's back and arms are the 'frame' in which the woman is held; a well-structured frame is essential for smooth dancing and good leading.

THE HAND POSITION

The man's left hand position as he starts to take up hold

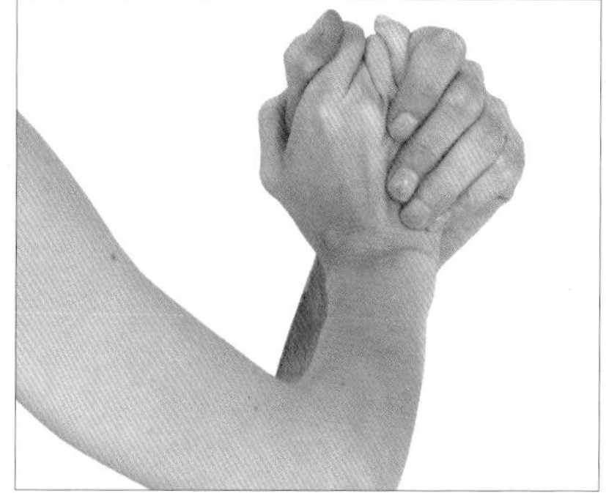

The man's left and woman's right hand hold

on the dance floor

There are a few basic rules that all couples need to know before they start dancing.

taking a step: A step is not only the positioning of the foot but also the subsequent transfer of weight, unless otherwise indicated.

FEET POSITIONS

The slightly offset position of the dancers allows them to move without treading on each others feet

direction of flow: All dancers travel in an overall anti-clockwise direction around the dance floor, irrespective of where they happen to be facing or moving during any individual step.

orientation: All dancers in couples orientate themselves using the nearest wall, the centre line of the room parallel to this wall, and diagonal lines, also known as zigs and zags. In this book, a zig is an imaginary line that travels, with the flow, from the centre line diagonally towards the wall; a zag is an imaginary line that travels, with the flow, from the wall diagonally towards the centre line. Normally the zig and zag are at a 45-degree angle to the wall or the centre line, but the angle can be increased or decreased to provide respectively lesser or greater travel around the floor.

corners: As they meet a corner, dancers re-orientate themselves using the new wall. There is then a new centre line, and the zigs and zags will travel between the new wall and the new centre line.

feet positions: When used, these are descriptions of one foot in relation to the other foot. 'Left foot forwards' therefore means 'left foot' forwards on the same line as the 'right foot' and not just 'generally forward' to avoid confusion: for example, 'diagonally forward' might otherwise mean 'generally forward' as well.

go with the flow

The special *Flowmotion* images used in this book have been created to ensure you see the whole of each dance sequence. In ballroom dancing the basic movement is always anti-clockwise, so these are shown running from right to left, except in one or two instances. Each sequence is labelled suitable for beginners or intermediate dancers by a coloured tab above the title. The captions along the bottom of the images provide additional information to help you perform the steps confidently. Below this, another layer of information explains when the steps are taken for each sequence, and the beat and timing, when appropriate. The photographs in bold show the position 'on the count', which helps beginners to visualise each step.

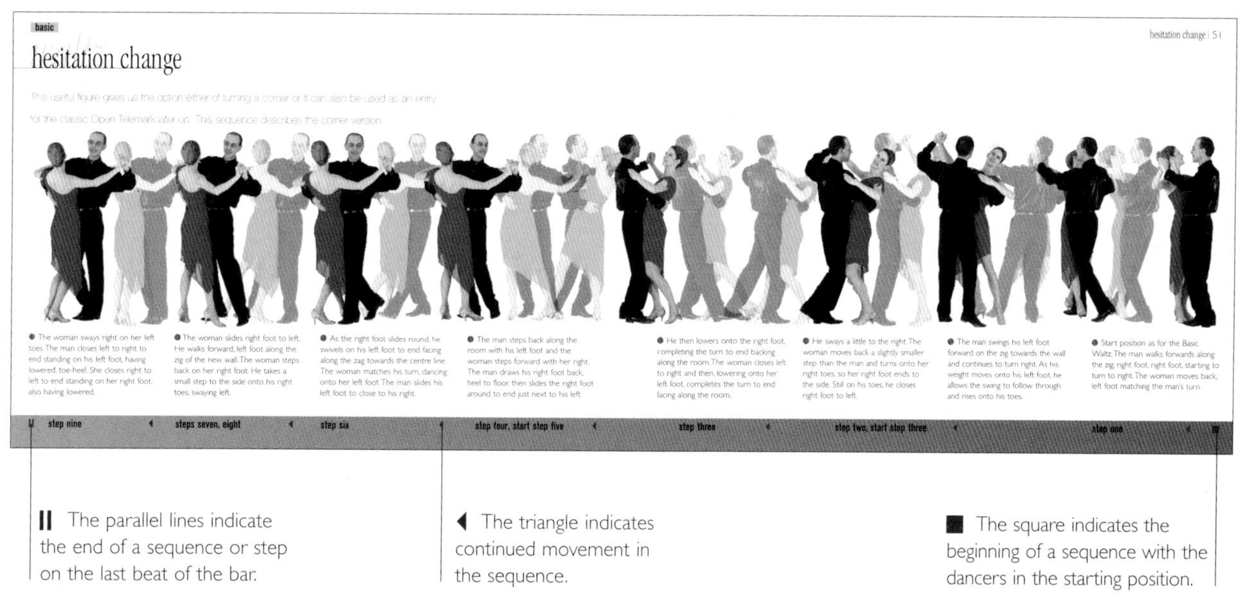

basic

hesitation change

hesitation change | 51

This useful figure gives us the option either of turning a corner or it can also be used as an entry for the classic Open Telemark later on. This sequence describes the corner version.

● The woman sways right on her left toes. The man closes left to right to end standing on his left foot, having lowered, toe-heel. She closes right to left to end standing on her right foot, also having lowered.

● The woman slides right foot to left. He walks forward, left foot along the zig of the new wall. The woman steps back on her right foot. He takes a small step to the side onto his right toes, swaying left.

● As the right foot slides round, he swivels on his left foot to end facing along the zag towards the centre line. The woman matches his turn, dancing onto her left foot. The man slides his left foot to close to his right.

● The man steps back along the room with his left foot and the woman steps forward with her right. The man draws his right foot back, heel to floor, then slides the right foot around to end just next to his left.

● He then lowers onto the right foot, completing the turn to end backing along the room. The woman closes left to right and then, lowering onto her left foot, completes the turn to end facing along the room.

● He sways a little to the right. The woman moves back a slightly smaller step than the man and turns onto her right toes, so her right foot ends to the side. Still on his toes, he closes right foot to left.

● The man swings his left foot forward on the zig towards the wall and continues to turn right. As his weight moves onto his left foot, he allows the swing to follow through and rises onto his toes.

● Start position as for the Basic Waltz. The man walks forwards along the zig, right foot, right foot, starting to turn to right. The woman moves back, left foot matching the man's turn.

II step nine ◂ steps seven, eight ◂ step six ◂ step four, start step five ◂ step three ◂ step two, start step three ◂ step one ◂ ■

II The parallel lines indicate the end of a sequence or step on the last beat of the bar.

◀ The triangle indicates continued movement in the sequence.

■ The square indicates the beginning of a sequence with the dancers in the starting position.

social foxtrot

the basic foxtrot

This is an easy, repeatable basic sequence to get first-time dancers comfortably and inconspicuously around the floor. The basic foxtrot forms the basis on which other moves can be added, and it can be danced to a wide variety of popular music.

● The woman matches the man as she dances side close, starting with her right foot to end standing on her left foot, feet together. The couple is now in the starting position again and can repeat the sequence.

● The man takes a small step to the side, turning from the zag onto the zig, and closes his right foot to his left to end standing on his right foot.

● The man ends standing on his right foot, the woman on her left. He walks back along the zag, left foot, then right and starts to turn towards the zig as he moves onto his right foot. She walks forwards, right foot, then left.

step eight, quick | **step seven, quick** | **steps five, six, slow, slow**

start

● Start in the Standard Ballroom Hold (see pp 12-13), but relax a little in the arms to enjoy this sociable dance. With feet together, the man stands on his right foot and the woman stands on her left foot.

step one, slow

● The man walks a normal step forwards with his left foot and the woman walks a normal step backwards with her right foot along the zig.

step two, slow

● The man walks forwards along the zig with his right foot starting to turn from the zig to the zag. The woman corresponds by walking back with her left foot, also starting to turn.

steps three, four, quick, quick

● Turning from the zig to the zag, the nan moves side onto his left foot, and ne woman takes a smaller side step n to her right. He closes his right oot to his left to end, and she closes er left foot to her right.

the rock turn to left

This is a simple move to add to your repertoire. Use all 12 steps for a complete rotation, as you might when waiting for floor traffic to clear ahead, or use just the first four steps to negotiate a corner.

● The man dances a short step side onto his left foot, then closes his right foot to his left, ending on his right foot. The woman dances a side close, starting with her right foot, ending on her left. Continue with the basic Foxtrot.

● The man walks forwards onto his left foot, curving to the left, then gently rocks back onto his right. The woman walks back, curving onto her right foot, before curving forwards onto her left foot.

● The man dances a short step side onto his left foot, then closes his right foot to his left, to end standing on his right foot. The woman dances a side close, starting with her right foot, to end standing on her left foot.

steps eleven, twelve, quick, quick ◀ **steps nine, ten, slow, slow** ◀ **steps seven, eight, quick, quick**

● The man walks forwards onto his :ft foot, curving to the left, then ently rocks back onto his right. The voman walks back, curving onto her ght foot, before curving forwards nto her left foot.

◀ **steps five, six, slow, slow**

● The man dances a short step side onto his left foot, then closes his right foot to his left, to end standing on his right foot. The woman dances a side close, starting with her right foot, to end standing on her left foot.

◀ **steps three, four, quick, quick**

● He flexes his knee to absorb the forwards movement, leaving his right foot behind, then gently rocks back onto his right foot. The woman walks back, curving onto her right foot before curving forwards onto her left.

◀ **step two, slow**

● The man is standing on his right foot, and the woman on her left, feet together, having completed the basic Foxtrot sequence. The man walks forwards onto his left foot, in line with the woman, but curves to the left.

◀ **step one, slow** ■

the time step

social foxtrot

This is a fun variation to slow down the progress around a congested dance floor, or simply to enjoy the rhythm of the music. Dance it after any of your Foxtrot moves.

● Over these last two steps, the couple will turn a little to resume their normal alignment on the zig.

● The man steps side onto his right foot and taps his left foot next to his right foot. The woman steps side onto the left foot, and taps her right foot next to her left.

● Moving to his left and still square, the man dances side, close, side,tap. starting with his left foot and ends tapping with his right. The woman dances the normal opposite.

The man steps right foot sideways, and then taps or touches his left foot next to his right without weight. The woman steps left foot sideways, and then taps or touches her right foot to her left without weight.

The man steps left foot sideways and then taps or touches his right foot next to his left without weight. The woman steps right foot sideways and then taps her left foot next to her right without weight.

He then steps right foot forward, turning from the zig to end facing squarely to the wall. The woman corresponds by walking right foot, then left, with a little turn to end squarely to the wall.

As if having completed the basic Foxtrot sequence, the man should be standing on his right foot, and the woman on her left. Both of them should have their feet together. The man steps forwards onto his left foot.

steps five, six, quick, quick **step four, quick** **step three, quick** **step two, slow** **step one, slow**

turn to the right

social foxtrot

This is a useful and impressive move for turning corners. It has eight steps, and you can continue it by dancing the last four steps of the basic Foxtrot. Swaying from side to side, adds a slightly more lilting rhythm to the movement.

● Continue with steps five to eight of the Basic Foxtrot, or, having completed step six of the Turn to Right to end facing the wall, continue with the Time Step starting with step three.

● Turning from the zig to the zag, the man moves side onto his left foot and the woman moves a smaller side step onto her right. He closes his right foot to his left and the woman her left to her right.

● The man walks forwards with his right foot starting to curve a little to the right along the zig of the new wall. The woman walks back onto her left foot to match the man's movements.

● The woman walks forwards onto her right foot, leaving her left foot extended behind. From this position, she pivots clockwise on her right foot to end backing the zig of the new wal

steps seven, eight, quick, quick ◀ **step six, slow** ◀ **step five, slow**

● Close attention is required for this tep. The man steps back onto his left oot, keeping his right foot extended in ront. From this position he pivots lockwise on his left foot to end facing he zig of the new wall.

● He then dances side onto the left, and closes right foot to left, continuing to turn more strongly to end backing down the room. She dances side onto her right foot, closing left foot to right to end facing down the room.

● The man steps forwards, left foot, then right foot, starting to turn to the right. The woman corresponds by walking back right foot, then left foot, matching her partner.

● Having completed the basic Foxtrot, the man stands on his right foot and the woman on her left. Both have their feet together.

step five, slow **steps three, four, quick, quick** **steps one, two slow, slow** **starting position**

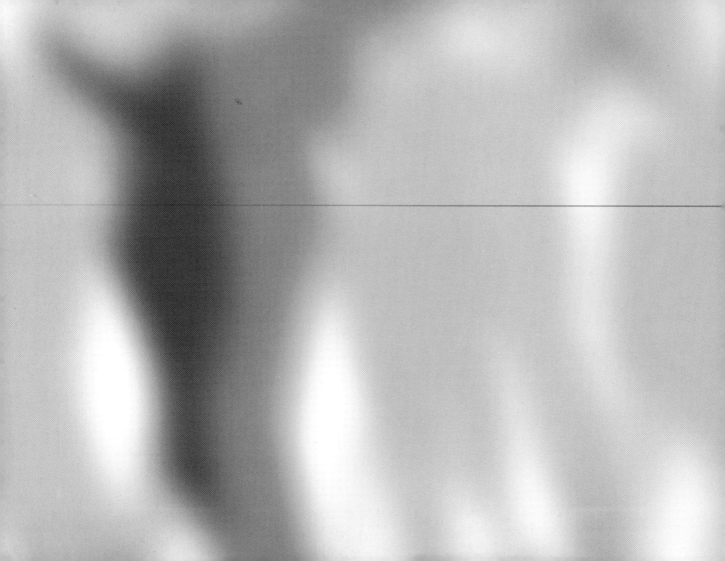

waltz

the basic waltz

This most romantic of dances is the traditional choice for weddings. An easy and repeatable basic pattern will move you effortlessly around the floor. The pattern forms the basis on which other attractive moves can be added later.

● The couple is now ready to repeat the Basic Waltz from the beginning. At the corner, the man increases the turn on step 7. Tip – whoever is moving back in to a turn takes a smaller step.

● With the same pattern, the man dances forward along the zig, walk, side, close, starting with his left foot and ending standing on his left foot.

● With the same pattern, the man turns from the zag to the zig dancing a backward walk, side, close, starting with his right foot and ending standing on his right foot. The woman dances the normal opposite.

steps eleven, twelve ◀ **steps nine, ten** ◀ **steps seven, eight**

● The woman dances the normal pposite. The man dances back along e zag, walk, side, close, starting left oot and ending standing on his eft foot.

● The woman dances the normal opposite. The three step pattern continues.

● The man dances a three step pattern comprising a forward walk, a side step, and a close starting with his right foot, turning from the zig to the zag and ending standing on his right foot.

● The dancers are standing, feet together, ready to move along the zig. The man is standing on his left foot and the woman her right.

steps five, six ◄ **steps three, four** ◄ **step two** ◄ **step one** ■

natural turn at a corner

Cornering can be a bit of a test in any dance, but here's one way of negotiating a corner while keeping the basic walk-side-close structure. Start as you approach the corner, having completed a basic Waltz sequence.

● The man closes his left foot to right, and lowers onto his left foot as he completes his turn to end facing along the zig of the new wall. The woman closes her right foot to her left and lowers onto her right foot.

● He then transfers his weight onto that foot, rising and swaying to the left as he turns on the toes of his right foot. The woman matches his turn, stepping side on to the toes of her left foot.

● The woman walks forward on her right foot, matching his turn. The man points his right foot towards the zig of the new wall.

● Still on his toes, the man closes his ght foot to his left and lowers onto ne right foot, completing the turn to nd backing along the room. The man valks back on his left foot, starting to ırn right.

● His weight moves onto the left foot, letting the swing follow through and rise onto the toes while the body sways a little to right. The woman moves back, a slightly smaller step than the man, turning onto the toes of her right foot so that it ends to the side.

● The woman moves back, left foot, matching the man's turn. The man walks forward along the zig, right foot, starting to turn to the right. He swings his left foot forward on the zig towards the wall, continuing to turn right.

● Start in the Standard Ballroom Hold (see pages 12–13), feet together, the man standing on his left foot on the zig and the woman on her right.

◀ **step three** ◀ **step two** ◀ **step one** **starting position** ■

outside change

The outside change is a great floorcraft move to help you by-pass other floor traffic that has halted ahead of you. It is also useful for extending the basic Waltz pattern if needed for a good approach to a corner.

● They are now ready to continue with the Basic Waltz, with one major difference. The man will take the first step of the following move with his right foot outside his partner's right foot before continuing as normal.

● The man points his left foot along the zig and lowers sideways onto his left foot. The woman lowers sideways onto her right foot.

● The man walks back along the zag, left foot; she walks forward, right foot. He now rises on his toes, steps back with his right foot, starting to turn left. The woman corresponds, rising onto her toes, and forward onto her left foot

● Completing the turn from the zig ɔ the zag, the man closes his right ɔot to his left, and the woman her ɛft to her right. Both lower onto the ıll foot. The man ends standing on his ght foot, and the woman on her left.

● The man moves side, turning from the zig to the zag, rising onto the toes of his left foot, swaying a little to the right. The woman corresponds, moving side onto her right foot, also starting to turn rise and sway.

● He takes a normal forward walk with his right foot., she takes a backwards walk with her left foot along the zig.

● Start in the Standard Ballroom Hold, with feet together. The man stands on his left foot on the zig, and the woman on her right.

outside change to promenade

In this sequence, the outside change is used in conjunction with the Promenade position. Once in Promenade position, you have the possibility of a range of exciting new moves to enjoy learning and dancing.

● Her body opens up as she lowers side, small step, toe-heel, onto her right foot so that it is pointing along the zag. They are now ready to carry out 'through the middle' as they travel along the floor.

● As the man moves to the 'promenade' position, the woman keeps her head up and turns it from left to right to end looking along the floor.

● There is almost a brief hover before the man lowers to the side, small step, toe-heel, onto his left foot, turning a little to an open, or 'promenade', position so that his left foot is pointing along the zig.

● The man now rises on his toes as he steps back with his right foot, starting to turn left. The woman corresponds by rising onto her toes a she moves forwards onto her left foo but she does not turn.

The man walks back along the zag, ft foot, and the woman walks ›rwards, right foot.

tep four

● Completing the turn from the zig to the zag, the man closes his right foot to his left, and the woman closes her left foot to her right. Both lower onto the full foot. He ends standing on his right foot and she ends on her left.

step three

● The man moves to the side, starting to turn from the zig to the zag and rising onto his left toes, swaying a little to the right. The woman moves side onto her right foot, also starting to turn, rise and sway.

step two

● Start in the Standard Ballroom Hold, feet together. The man stands on his left foot on the zig, the woman on her right. He walks forward with his right foot, the woman a backward walk with her left along the zig.

starting position, step one

chassé from promenade

Here, the promenade is used in conjunction with the chassé to propel you powerfully but gracefully along the room in a syncopated but flowing move, overtaking other floor traffic and increasing your progress around the floor. The chassé is a side-close-side element.

● This step will be the first step of the next move and has to be modified because of the slightly different relative body positions. The picture above shows how the man will lead the woman to dance into the next move.

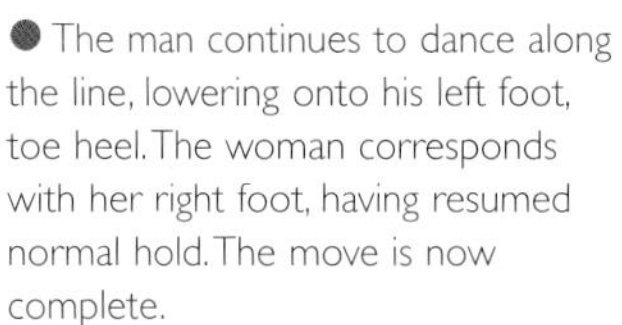

● The man continues to dance along the line, lowering onto his left foot, toe heel. The woman corresponds with her right foot, having resumed normal hold. The move is now complete.

● The woman closes her left foot to her right foot, remaining on her toes, and closing her head to its normal position and right side to the man.

● She starts to turn her head and right side towards the man. Steps two and three are taken together in one beat of music. The man closes his right foot to his left foot, remaining on his toes.

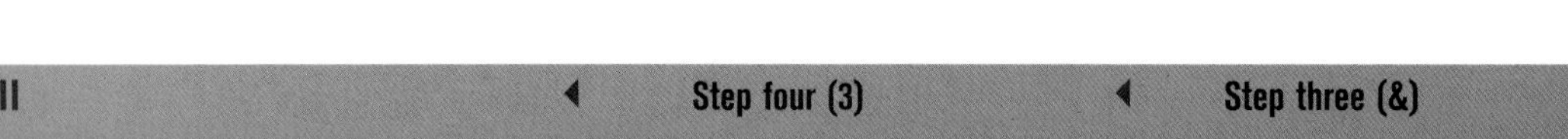

Step four (3)

Step three (&)

Step two (2)

His body remains facing the zig
though he is travelling along the
oom. The woman swings her right
ot forwards, along the same line
ong the room, and moves onto her
ght toes.

● The man and woman walk 'through the middle' along the room, man right foot, woman left. He then swings his left foot forwards along the same line along the room and moves onto the toes of his left foot.

● The man's left side and the woman's right side are slightly open – further apart than the man's right and the woman's left sides. Both are looking along the room.

● Start in the promenade position (see end of previous move). The man is standing on his left foot, feet apart, and the woman on her right, feet apart.

whisk and chassé

The whisk is a great floorcraft figure. It can be used instead of steps 10–12 of the Basic Waltz to change direction without interrupting the flow of the dance, and then move along the floor into clearer space

● The man continues to dance along the the line, lowering onto his left foot, toe heel. She corresponds with her right foot to finish, having resumed normal hold. The move is now complete.

● The woman closes her left foot to her right, remaining on her toes, and closing her head towards its normal position, right side of the man. Steps five and six are taken in one beat of music.

● She moves onto her right toes, starting to turn her head and right side towards the man. Steps five and six are taken together with one beat of music. The man closes his right foot to his left, remaining on his toes.

● The man then swings his left foot forwards along the same line along t room and moves onto his left toes. His body remains facing the zig. The woman swings her right foot forwarc along the same line along the room.

● She completes her turn onto the ag. As they complete the move, they nd in promenade position, both ooking along the floor. They walk hrough the middle' along the room, nan right foot, woman left.

● She also starts to arc her head over to her right. The man crosses his left foot behind his right, under his body, and lowers his weight, toe-heel, onto his foot. The woman corresponds with her right foot.

● The man walks forward, left foot, on the zig, and the woman back right. He moves side onto his right toes, still on the zig. The woman starts to turn onto the zag as she steps back diagonally onto her right toes.

● Start in the Standard Ballroom Hold, feet together. The man stands on his right foot on the zig and the woman on her left, having danced steps 1–9 of the Basic Waltz.

step five (2) **step four (1)** ◀ **step three (3)** **step two (2)** **step one (1)** ◀ **starting position** ■

three walks curving to the right

If you are ready to start your Basic Waltz pattern, but you notice another couple is blocking your path along the room, here's a stylish floorcraft figure to avoid them. Of course, it is an exciting move to enjoy anyway.

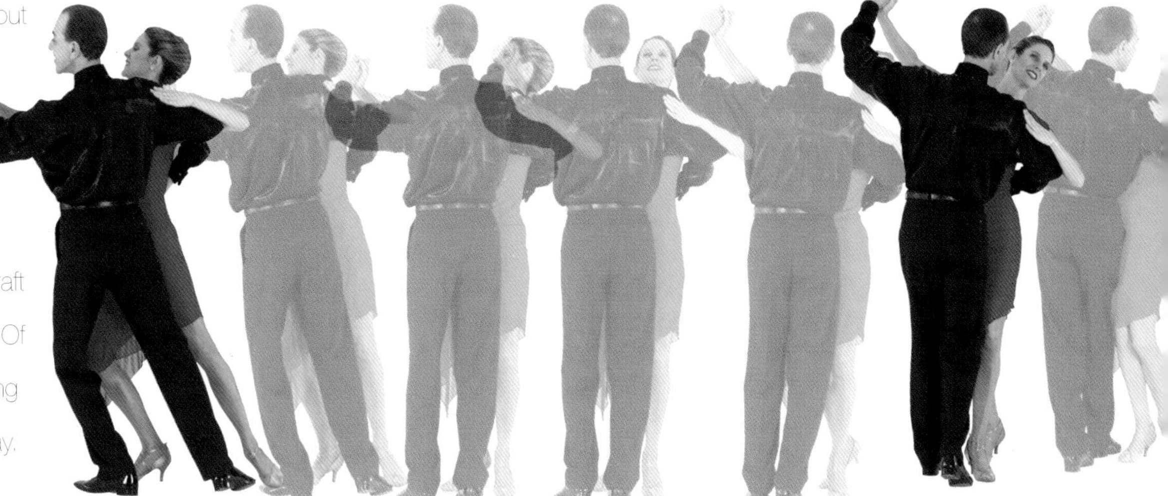

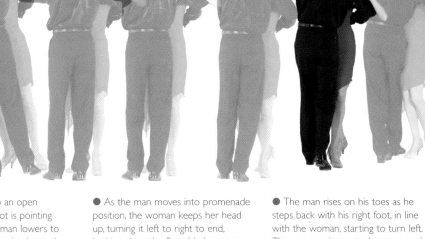

● They are now ready to dance 'through the middle' as they travel along the floor into a Chassé from promenade position.

● He turns a little to an open position so his left foot is pointing along the zig. The woman lowers to the side, small step, toe-heel, onto her right foot so it is pointing along the zag.

● As the man moves into promenade position, the woman keeps her head up, turning it left to right to end, looking along the floor. He lowers to the side, small step, toe-heel, onto his left foot.

● The man rises on his toes as he steps back with his right foot, in line with the woman, starting to turn left. The woman rises onto her toes as sh moves forwards onto her left foot, bu does not turn.

● The woman lowers, toe-heel, as she [t]akes a small step back, underneath [h]er body along the zag. The man walks [b]ack along the zag, left foot, and the [w]oman walks forwards, right foot, [o]utside the man's right side.

● To add style, the couple may sway a little towards the centre of the turn. He moves forward outside the woman's right side, lowering toe-heel onto his right foot, still curving right to end on the zag.

● The woman corresponds as she walks back onto her left foot. The man moves forwards onto his left toes, still curving to end square with the wall. The woman moves back onto her right toes, still curving.

● Start in the Standard Ballroom Hold, feet together. The man stands on his left foot on the zig, and the woman on her right. He curves to his right as he walks forwards onto his right foot.

hairpin from and to promenade

Life starts to get exciting. You have moved into Promenade position and are ready to drive along the floor when suddenly another couple blocks your path and you have to perform a hairpin turn to avoid them. This is how the professionals do it.

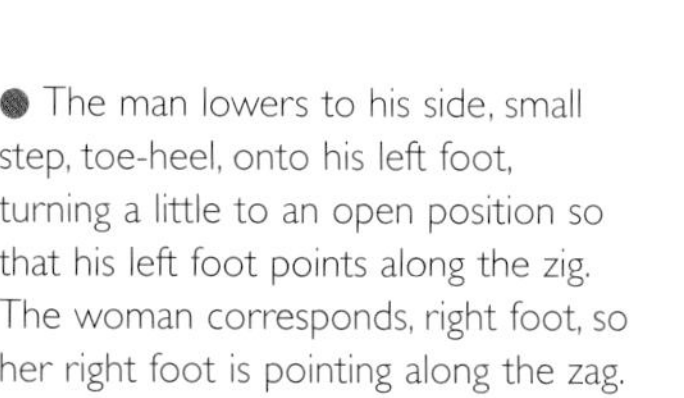

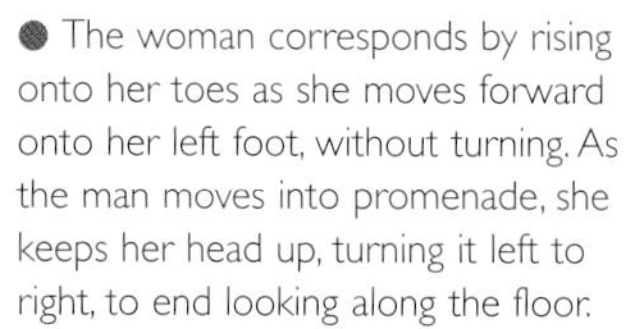

● The man lowers to his side, small step, toe-heel, onto his left foot, turning a little to an open position so that his left foot points along the zig. The woman corresponds, right foot, so her right foot is pointing along the zag.

● The woman corresponds by rising onto her toes as she moves forward onto her left foot, without turning. As the man moves into promenade, she keeps her head up, turning it left to right, to end looking along the floor.

● The man walks back along the zag, left foot, and the woman walks forward, right foot, outside the man's right. He rises onto his toes as he steps back with his right foot in line with the woman. He starts to turn left.

● He lowers, toe-heel, onto his right foot, still curving to the right to end on the zag. The woman lowers toe-heel, as she takes a small step back, underneath her body, along the zag.

The woman corresponds, moving her head from the promenade position, right, to the close hold position, left. The man moves forwards outside the woman's right side.

To change direction towards the wall, the man closes the woman from promenade to close hold, lifts strongly onto his left toes, and sways to the right.

As they continue along the line, the man moves onto his left toes, and the woman onto her right toes. With the way ahead blocked, he decelerates, absorbing the movement by flexing his left knee, and swaying to the left.

In promenade position, the man and woman move along the line between them. He walks forwards and across with his right foot, and the woman walks forward and across with her left.

step two, start step three | **step two** | **start step two** | **step one**

intermediate

waltzes

hover telemark to chassé

The Hover Telemark is one of the classiest floorcraft figures as well as changing direction and moving in to the useful Promenade position. It has great panache, a lot of shape, and is easy to lead.

step five (2)

● The man then swings his left foot forwards along the same line along the room, and moves onto his left toes. The woman does the same but with her right foot, starting to turn her head and right side towards the man.

step six (and)

● Steps five and six are taken in one beat of music. The man closes his right foot to left, staying on his toes. The woman closes left to right, on her toes, and closes her head to its normal position, right side to the man.

step seven (3)

● The man continues to dance along the line, lowering onto his left foot, toe-heel. The woman corresponds with her right foot, having resumed normal hold. The move is now complete.

step eight

● This step will be the first step of the next move and has to be modified because of the slightly different relative body positions. The last picture shows how the man will lead the woman to dance into the next move.

● The woman lowers side, small step, oe-heel, onto her right foot so it is ointing along the zag. They then ance 'through the middle' as they avel along the floor, man right foot, oman left.

● They are now ready for the promenade position. The man lowers to the side, small step, toe-heel, onto his left foot in promenade position so that his left foot is pointing along the zig.

● The man turns his body to the left, walks forwards, left foot along the zig. The woman walks back with her right. The man closes his right foot to his left, rises onto his toes, moving his head right to left. The woman corresponds.

● Start on the zig in the Standard Ballroom Hold. The couple have their feet closed. The man is standing on his right foot and the woman on her left, having completed nine steps of the Basic Waltz.

natural spin turn 1

This impressive-looking move has become the international standard method of turning a corner in the Waltz and, incidentally, the Quickstep. The spin may seem a little awkward while you are taking your time to master it, but it is well worth investing the effort.

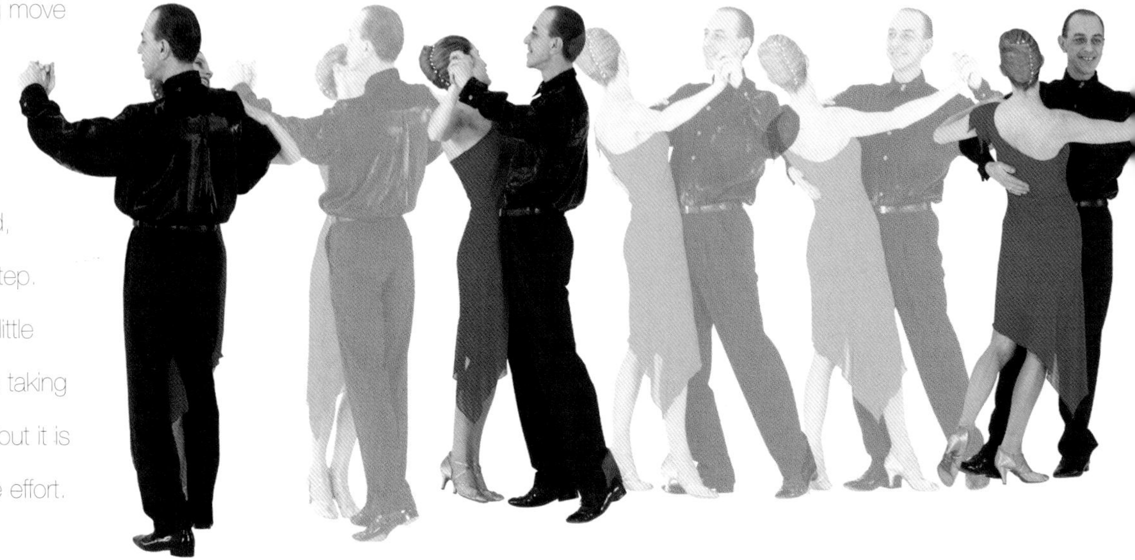

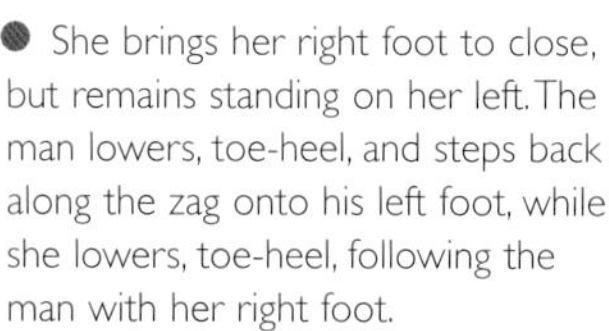

● She brings her right foot to close, but remains standing on her left. The man lowers, toe-heel, and steps back along the zag onto his left foot, while she lowers, toe-heel, following the man with her right foot.

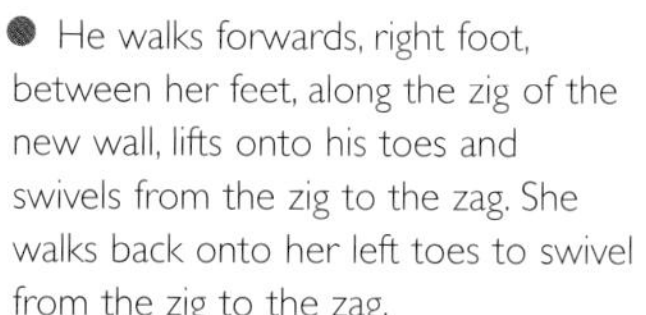

● He walks forwards, right foot, between her feet, along the zig of the new wall, lifts onto his toes and swivels from the zig to the zag. She walks back onto her left toes to swivel from the zig to the zag.

● He turns right to face the zig of the new wall. She walks forwards onto her right foot, starting to turn right, leaving her left foot extended behind. She swivels to the right on her right toes, to end backing the zig of the new wall.

● She completes the turn to end facing along the room. The man steps back onto his left foot, turning it in a little, knees together, left knee flexed, and right foot extended straight in front. He swivels on his left heel.

Still on his toes, the man closes ght foot to left, then lowers onto his ght foot to end, backing along the om. She closes her left foot to her ght, then lowers onto her left foot.

● As he does so, he allows the swing to follow through and rise onto his toes, swaying a little to the right. The woman takes a slightly smaller step back and turns onto her right toes. Her right foot ends to the side.

● The woman moves back, left foot matching the man's turn. He swings his left foot forwards on the zig towards the wall, and continues to turn right. He moves his weight onto the left foot.

● Start as for the Basic Waltz. Allow yourself plenty of room ahead as you dance the Natural Turn Spin as you approach the corner. The man walks forwards along the zig, right foot, starting to turn right.

step three ◄ **step two** ◄ **step one** ■

natural spin turn 2

After turning the corner with a stylish natural spin turn, continue with an uninterrupted flow into step seven of the Basic Waltz, but this time along the new wall.

● They are now ready to continue with the Basic Waltz or even try the Three Walks Curving to Right.

step twelve ◀

● The man closes his left foot to right to end, standing on his left foot, having lowered toe-heel. The woman corresponds by closing her right foot to her left to end, standing on her right, also having lowered toe-heel.

step eleven ◀

● The man takes a small step to the side onto the toes of his right foot, swaying to left. The woman takes a small side step onto her left toes, swaying to the right.

step ten ◀

● She also lowers toe-heel and sway to her left. The man walks forwards, left foot along the zig, and the woma walks back onto her right foot. (Option: substitute steps 10–12 and go straight into the Hover Telemark.)

The man closes his right foot to his ft to end standing on his right foot, ving lowered toe-heel, swaying to e right and facing along the zig. The oman closes her left foot to her ght, to end standing on her left foot.

● The man takes a small step to the side onto the toes of his left foot, pointing along the zig, swaying to the right. The woman steps side onto the toes of her right foot, also turning and swaying to the left.

● The man walks back on his right foot, starting to curve on the zig. The woman walks forward with her right foot, also starting to turn.

● The couple is now in the starting position.

tep nine ◀ **step eight** **step seven** ◀ ■

hesitation change

This useful figure gives us the option either of turning a corner or it can also be used as an entry for the classic Open Telemark later on. This sequence describes the corner version.

● The woman sways right on her left toes. The man closes left to right to end standing on his left foot, having lowered, toe-heel. She closes right to left to end standing on her right foot, also having lowered.

● The woman slides right foot to left. He walks forward, left foot along the zig of the new wall. The woman steps back on her right foot. He takes a small step to the side onto his right toes, swaying left.

● As the right foot slides round, he swivels on his left foot to end facing along the zag towards the centre line. The woman matches his turn, dancing onto her left foot. The man slides his left foot to close to his right.

● The man steps back along the room with his left foot and the woman steps forward with her right. The man draws his right foot back, heel to floor, then slides the right foo around to end just next to his left.

II **step nine** ◄ **steps seven, eight** ◄ **step six** ◄ **step four, start step five**

He then lowers onto the right foot, ›mpleting the turn to end backing ›ng the room. The woman closes left › right and then, lowering onto her ft foot, completes the turn to end cing along the room.

● He sways a little to the right. The woman moves back a slightly smaller step than the man and turns onto her right toes, so her right foot ends to the side. Still on his toes, he closes right foot to left.

● The man swings his left foot forward on the zig towards the wall and continues to turn right. As his weight moves onto his left foot, he allows the swing to follow through and rises onto his toes.

● Start position as for the Basic Waltz. The man walks forwards along the zig, right foot, right foot, starting to turn to right. The woman moves back, left foot matching the man's turn.

step three ◄ **step two, start step three** ◄ **step one** ◄ ■

waltz

open telemark and chassé

When the hesitation change is danced along the side of a room, not at a corner, the final three steps can be replaced by this beautiful sequence. Initially, this move takes us across the flow towards the centre line of the room before turning into promenade. It can then be followed by any of your promenade moves. In this sequence we show the standard Chassé.

● The man continues to dance along the line, lowering onto his left foot, toe heel. The woman corresponds with her right foot and having resumed normal hold. The move is now complete.

● The man closes his right foot to his left and remains on his toes. The woman closes her left foot to her right, remaining on her toes. She closes her head towards its normal position and right side to the man.

● He swings his left foot forwards along the same line and moves onto his left toes. His body remains facing the zig. She swings her right foot forwards along the same line and moves onto her right toes.

II step seven (3) ◀ **step six (&)** ◀ **step five (2)** ◀

The woman lowers side, toe-heel, ıto her right foot in promenade ɔsition. The couple is now looking ɔng the room. The man and woman alk 'through the middle' along the ·om, man right foot, woman left.

● The woman lifts onto her left toes. Note the head positions, sway and body shaping. The man continues to turn to his left and takes a small step, lowering side, toe-heel, onto his left foot, with foot pointing along the zig.

● She draws her left foot back, heel in contact with the floor, to close her left foot to right. With left foot now tucked in against her right, and her heel still in contact with the floor, she continues turning on her right heel.

● The man walks forwards, left foot, starting to turn left, while the woman walks back, right foot. The man swings his right side and foot forwards past the woman and moves onto his right toes, continuing to turn to the left.

waltz

hover from promenade

We have already seen how the Hairpin can be used as an emergency avoidance figure when in promenade position. The Hover from Promenade is a gentler option which absorbs the movement rather than deflecting it, as in the Hairpin. Continue with the Reverse Whisk.

● The woman steps forwards against the flow, lowering toe heel, onto her left foot. The dancers have now haltered their progress and are ready to travel momentarily against the flow and continue in the Reverse Whisk.

● The woman's head reverts to its normal left position. The man now lowers, toe-heel, as he moves back onto his right foot, which has remained behind.

● The man overturns to the left wh swaying to the right to absorb the flow of movement. This is felt as a gentle upward sweep. As the woman weight is neutralized over her feet, they naturally come together.

• The woman swings her right foot ›rwards along the same line along the ›om and moves onto the toes of her ght foot. She starts to turn her head ıd right side towards the man.

• The man then swings his left foot forwards along the same line along the room and moves onto the toes of his left foot. The man's body remains facing the zig although he is travelling along the room.

• The man and woman walk through the middle of the room, man right foot, woman left foot.

• Start in the promenade position, ready to move along the room as if for a Chassé.

reverse whisk from hover promenade

This is a variation of the Whisk you have already encountered, but it is modified to take in to account the different entry position from the Hover Promenade. The combination of these two moves gives a graceful, but sweeping elegance to the overall effect. This sequence runs from left to right.

● The couple has just completed the Hover Promenade. The man is standing back on his right foot and the woman is forward on her left foot.

● The man moves back against the flow, taking his left foot underneath his body.

● The woman moves forwards against the flow, slightly across herself, taking her right foot outside the man's right side as she prepares to turn to the right.

The man continues to move along e same line, against the flow, onto e toes of his right foot. Note that e man's body position does not ter.

● The woman moves forward against the flow onto the toes of her left foot, then turns to right on her left foot. As usual, the woman's head moves from left to right as she moves towards a promenade position.

● The man crosses his left foot behind his right, under his body, and lowers his weight, toe heel, onto the foot. The woman corresponds with her right foot, completing her turn onto the zag.

● As the move is completed, the couple will end in promenade position and both will be looking along the floor. The dancers are now able to continue into any of the movements from promenade position.

advanced

checked natural turn with a reverse pivot and open telemark

As you enter any move that turns to the right, the floor traffic may force you to change your plan. Here is an excellent Plan 'B' that can be danced with verve and vivacity. This combination has powerful dynamics that provide great flexibility and give a great feeling to your dancing.

● Pivoting on his right toes, he takes a small step lowering side, toe-heel, on to his left foot, so it is pointing to the wall along the zig. She lowers side, toe-heel, onto her right foot in promenade position. They look along the room.

● The woman draws her left foot back, heel in contact with the floor, to close her left foot to her right foot. She continues turning on her right heel, matching the man, then lifts onto the toes of her left foot.

● He walks forward left foot, starting to turn left, while the woman walks back right foot. The man swings his right side and foot forward past the woman and moves onto his left toes, continuing to turn left.

● His left foot is extended in front, ‹nees together. The woman moves ›rward, lowering, toe-heel, onto her ›ft foot, knees together and matching ›e man's turn. Her head resumes its ›ormal left position.

● The turn is now checked. The woman may move her head over to the right. He curves back turning strongly to the left lowering, toe-heel, onto his right foot to end on the zag facing the centre line of the room.

● As his weight moves onto the left foot, he follows through and rises onto the toes, while his body sways a little to right. She takes a smaller step back and turns onto her right toes so that her right foot ends to the side.

● The man walks forward along the zig, right foot, starting turn to right. The woman moves back, left foot matching the man's turn. He swings his left foot forward on the zig towards the wall, continuing to turn right

step three ◄ **start step three** ◄ **step two** **step one, start step two** ■

waltz

whisk and wing

As you become more adept at joining moves together, you will want to try even more interesting combinations of figures. Here is one such stylish but practical combination.

step six

● The woman lowers, toe-heel, forward on to her left foot outside the man's left side and moves her head over to her left. They are now ready to continue with the chassé to right and outside change.

step five

● The woman moves her right side and foot forward onto the toes around the man. The man closes his left foot to his right. He continues turning left until he is on the zag facing towards the centre line of the room.

step four

● The man stays on his right foot in the centre of turn, continuing to turn left, drawing his left foot towards his right without weight and guiding the woman around him.

● The man and the woman walk
rough the middle along the room,
an right foot, woman left. The couple
arts to turn left. The woman will feel
at she is starting to walk around the
an, left foot.

tep three

● The woman corresponds with her right foot, completing her turn on to the zag. As the move is completed, the couple will end in promenade position and both will be looking along the room.

step two

● Additionally, the woman starts to arc her head over to her right. The man crosses his left foot behind his right, under his body, and lowers his weight, toe heel, on to the foot.

step one

● The man walks forward, left foot on the zig, and the woman back right. He moves side on to his right toes, still on the zig, while the woman starts to turn onto the zag as she steps diagonally back onto her right toes.

chassé to right and outside change

Having danced the Whisk and Wing, the dancers are now able to continue straight into this move to complete a favourite combination of figures that have become an enduring classic combination.

● The couple is now ready to continue with the Basic Waltz or any of the moves that start from this position, but ensuring that the next step for the man is taken outside the woman's right side.

● The man continues his turn to the left and lowers side, toe-heel, onto his left foot on the zig. The woman corresponds, turning to the left and lowering side, toe-heel, on to her right foot.

● The woman moves forward, right foot outside the man's right side. He moves back along the line onto his right toes, starting to turn left. She moves forward onto her left toes, matching the man's turn.

step eight ◀ **step seven (3)** ◀ **step six (2)** ◀

The man lowers, toe-heel, as he oves along the line on to his right ot. The woman lowers, toe-heel, as e moves along the line onto her left ot. He steps back, left foot beneath s body and along the line.

● The man closes his left foot to the right foot, still on the toes and continues to turn to back along the zig. The woman closes her right foot to her left foot, still on the toes, and matching the man's turn.

● Still moving along the room, the man steps side on to his right toes, turning to back the wall. The woman moves side on to the toes of her left foot. Steps two and three are taken during the same beat of music.

● As he starts to move along the room, the man moves forward onto his left foot outside the woman's left side, turning slightly to his left. The woman moves back onto her right foot.

step five (1) **step four (3)** **steps two (2), three (&)** **step one (1)** ◄

pre-intermediate

waltz

the weave

By overturning the Outside Change to Promenade Position, or turning the Whisk a little to the left, you can continue with the Weave. With no closing steps, the Weave is an internationally standard figure that creates a great sense of flow as the dancers move around the room. If danced from a promenade position, note the adjustment of turn required.

● The couple is now ready to continue with the Basic Waltz or any other move starting from this position. The man's first step must be taken outside the woman's right side.

● The man continues his turn left and lowers side, toe-heel, onto his left foot on the zig. The woman corresponds, turning left and lowering side, toe-heel, onto her right foot.

● The man moves back along the lin onto the toes of his right foot, startin to turn to left. The woman moves forward onto the toes of the left foot matching the man's turn.

The man steps back, underneath
e body and along the line, left foot.
ıe woman moves forward right foot
ıtside the man's right side.

The man moves his right foot to the side and slightly back, lowering toe-heel, to end almost backing along the room. She corresponds, lowering side and slightly forward onto her left foot, to end almost facing along the room.

The man moves forward, between the woman's feet, onto his left toes, still turning left. The woman steps past the man, moving as she turns to face him, moving side and slightly back onto the toes of her right foot.

From the promenade position, the couple 'walk through the middle', the man right foot, the woman left foot, starting to turn along the zag towards the centre line of the room.

advanced

waltz

passing natural and outside spin

This is a terrific move with a great feel and a great deal of panache. It needs a good sense of timing but practice is rewarded with one of the classiest of the classic moves. Dance it after an Open Telemark.

● He rises side on to his left toes, closes right foot to the left and lowers, toe heel, onto his right foot. She rises side onto her right toes, closes her left foot to right and lowers, toe-heel, onto her left foot.

● The couple now dance steps 1–3 of the Basic Waltz but turning more strongly. He curves forward onto his right foot, aiming towards the zag. She corresponds, matching the turn and stepping back onto her left foot.

● She closes her left foot to right ar rises onto her toes as she performs the spin. He continues the spin, stepping side and lowering, toe-heel, onto his left foot. She lowers, toe-he as she steps onto her right foot.

step nine | step eight | step seven | step six

● From the promenade position, the couple walk forward and across themselves, through the middle and along the zig; man right foot, woman left foot.

● The man swings his left side and foot forward, turning across the zig, rising onto his left toes, and ending backing the zig. The woman continues forward along the zig, onto the toes of her right foot.

● The man lowers, toe-heel, as he steps back along the zig onto his right foot. The woman lowers, toe-heel, as she steps forward, left foot, along the zig. He steps back, left foot with the toe turned in, starting to turn right.

● The woman moves forward outside ˀhe man's right side, starting to turn ˀight. He moves forward, slightly across ˀimself and outside the woman's right, ˀide, rising onto his right foot. This is a ˀtrong step.

step one ◄ **step two** ◄ **step three, step four** ◄ **ˀteps five** ◄

quickstep

the basic quickstep

Fun, lively and vivacious, this is one of the faster flowing ballroom dances. It is a great way of enjoying some classic swing music. The Quickstep is a syncopated dance using Slow and Quick counts. A Slow is danced over two beats of the music and a Quick on a single beat.

● You can now repeat the Basic Quickstep. As the man walks forward into the next move, he will take the first step of that move forward outside the woman's right side.

● The man moves side along the room lowering, toe-heel, onto his left foot, pointing along the zig. The woman lowers, toe-heel, onto her right foot.

● The woman corresponds by moving side onto the right toes. The man closes his right foot to his left, st on his toes, continuing to turn onto the zig. The woman closes her left foc to her right, matching the man's turn.

step eight, slow **step seven, quick** **step six, quick**

The man steps his right foot back, ɔng the zag as he starts to turn left. ɿe woman walks forward with her ft foot, matching the man's turn He oves side along the room onto his ft toes, turning square to the wall.

● The man lowers, toe-heel, onto his left foot as he walks back along the zag. The woman lowers, toe heel, onto her right foot as she walks forward along the zag.

● She corresponds by moving side on to her right toes. The man closes his right foot to his left, still on his toes, turning onto the zag. The woman closes her left foot to her right, matching the man's turn.

● Start as for the Basic Waltz. The man walks forward right foot on the zig, turning right. The woman steps back onto her left foot. He moves side along the room onto his left toes, turning square to the wall.

tep five, slow ◄ **step four, slow** ◄ **step three, quick** ◄ **step two, quick** ◄ **step one, slow** ◄

natural turn around a corner

quickstep

This is probably the easiest move to get you around a corner in Quickstep, but it is not the same as the Natural Turn Around a Corner in the Waltz. Rather, it is similar to the Hesitation Change in the Waltz, but quicker and the last step is a walking step.

● The woman matches the man's turn as she dances side on to her left foot. The man transfers his weight onto his right foot, then walks forward, left foot, along the zig of the new wall and the woman back right.

● The man draws his right foot back, then slides the right foot around to end next to the left foot with the feet a little apart. As the foot slides around, the man swivels on his left foot to end facing along the zig of the new wall.

● The man steps back along the room with his left foot and the woman forward with her right. It is good practice for the man to release his right toes so that his heel in contact with the floor.

step six, quick ◄ **step five, slow** ◄

● The dancers's feet are apart, having danced, for example, the Basic Quickstep. The man is standing on his left foot on the zig, and the woman is standing on her right foot.

● The man walks forward along the zig, right foot outside the woman's right side, starting to turn to the right. The woman moves back, left foot matching the man's turn. He swings his left foot forward on the zig to the wall

● As the man's weight moves onto his left foot, he rises onto his toes, and sways a little to right. The woman steps back, slightly smaller than the man's, and turns onto her right toes so that her right foot ends to the side.

Still on the toes, the man closes his ght foot to his left, then lowers onto s right foot, completing the turn to d backing along the room. She rresponds by closing her left foot to r right, lowering onto her left foot.

step one, slow ◀ **step two, quick** ◀ **step three, quick** ◀ **tep four, slow**

chassé and lockstep

quickstep

The Lockstep follows the second half of the Basic Quickstep but has about half the length of the whole Basic Quickstep pattern. This makes it ideal as a spacer figure to give you the perfect entry into your corner move. It can also be used between two sets of Basic Quickstep for variety.

● The couple is now ready to continue into either the Basic Quickstep or a corner move, ensuring that the man takes the next step right foot forward outside the woman's right side.

● The man crosses his right foot loosely behind his left foot. The woman crosses her left foot loosely in front of her right foot. He moves foward, lowering toe-heel onto his left foot. She corresponds with her right.

● The man swings his left foot forward along the room onto the toe while the woman swings her right foc back along the room onto the toes.

II ◄ step four, slow ◄ step three, quick step two, quick

The woman lowers, toe-heel, onto r right foot. He moves forward right ɔt along the room outside the ɔman's right side. She moves back ɔng the room onto her right foot.

● The man closes his right foot to his left. The woman closes her left foot to her right, matching the man's turn. The man moves side along the room lowering, toe-heel, onto his left foot, pointing along the zig.

● The man moves side along the room onto his left toes, turning square to the wall. The woman corresponds by moving side onto her right toes.

● Having completed steps one to four of the Basic Quickstep, the man walks back, right foot, along the zag, starting to turn left. The woman matches the man's turn by walking forwards onto her left foot.

ep one, slow ◄ step eight, slow ◄ step seven, quick ◄ step six, quick step five, slow ◄ ■

natural hairpin and running finish

This is where you really start to feel the dynamic movement of the Quickstep as you flow freely along the floor at an exhilarating speed. Make sure the floor ahead is clear, to avoid a collision! Danced with care, this is a fabulous figure to enjoy.

● You can now repeat the Basic Quickstep. As the man walks forward in to the next move, he will takes the first step of that move forward outside the woman's right side.

● Facing along the room, he swings his left side forward, lowering, toe heel, onto left foot. She corresponds by matching the man's turn to end backing along the room and lowering her right foot back, toe-heel.

● The woman reaches forward along the room with the toes of her left foot and, matching the man's turn and swaying to right, rises onto the toes of her left foot.

● The man extends his right foot along the room, turning to point the toes along the zag towards the centre line. Swaying to the left, he rises onto his right toes.

step six, quick ◀ step five, quick ◀

The woman lowers, toe-heel, as she
ɜps back, underneath her body
:ing along the room. Relaxing into
e knees, he moves back onto his left
ot and she moves forwards, right
ot outside man's right side.

● The man moves forward outside the woman's right side, lowering toe-heel onto his right foot, still curving to the right to end backing along the room.

● The man moves forward onto his left toes and the woman moves back onto her right toes. To add style, the couple may sway a little towards the centre of the turn.

● The man curves to right as he walks forward onto his right foot outside the womanís right side. The woman corresponds as she walks back onto her left foot.

:ep four, slow ◀ **step three, quick** ◀ **step two, quick** **step one, slow** ◀ **start position** ■

back lock and running finish

quickstep

The Running Finish is such a great favourite that we will now start to develop a variety of options to give it even more zest. In this sequence, we introduce the Lockstep but, this time, it's the man who will be travelling backwards.

● You can now repeat the Basic Quickstep. As the man walks forward into the next move, he will takes the first step of that move forward outside the woman's right side.

● He swings his left side forward and moves forward, lowering, toe-heel, onto his left foot. She matches the man's turn to end backing along the room and lowering her right foot back, toe-heel.

step seven, quick

● He continues, swaying to the left and rising onto his right toes. The woman reaches forward along the room with her left, matching the man's turn and swaying to the right, rising onto her left toes.

step six, quick

● The man continues to move back along the room onto his left foot an the woman moves forward with her right foot outside the man's right sid He extends his right foot along the room, pointing his toes along the za

The man moves back lowering, [toe]-heel, onto his right foot, and the [w]oman moves forward, lowering, [toe]-heel, onto her left foot. The couple [is] now ready to continue in to the [ru]nning finish.

● Meanwhile, the woman swings her left foot forwards along the room onto her toes. Still on his toes, he crosses his left foot loosely in front of his right. She crosses her right foot loosely behind her left.

● The man moves back along the room onto his left foot. The woman moves forward, right foot along the room outside the man's right side.He swings his right foot back along the room onto his toes.

● Having danced the Hairpin, the man is backing along the room and is forward on his right foot outside the woman's right side. The woman is facing along the room and is back on her left foot.

[s]tep five slow ◄ step four, slow ◄ step three, quick ◄ step two, quick ◄ step one, slow ■

running finish, switch and running telemark

As we develop the Running Finish, we are now ready to include the Switch and another move, loved by competitors, called the Running Telemark. This will need some patience to master but a successful result will be well worth the effort.

● This ends the Quickstep section. It is one of the most demanding and enjoyable in all ballroom dancing.

● He moves forwards onto his right foot, swaying left. She matches the man, moving back onto her left toes. He swings left foot and side forwards, lowering toe-heel. She lowers toe-heel and steps back onto her right.

● He moves forward, right foot outside her right side. She moves back onto her left foot. He walks forward onto his left foot, swaying to the right and looking over her left shoulder. She steps back with right foot.

● He swings his left side forward, lowering, toe-heel, onto his left foot. She matches the man's turn and end backing along the room, lowering her right foot back, toe-heel. They are no ready for the Running Telemark.

steps eight, nine, quick ◀ step seven, slow step six, slow

The man leads the woman strongly
move onto his right side. He takes
small step forward along the room
to his right toes, and the woman
oves along the room onto the toes
her left foot. The turn continues.

● The man moves across himself along the room onto his left toes, outside the woman's left side. The woman steps back underneath herself, onto the toes of her right foot.

● He extends his right foot along the room, turning to point his toes along the zag towards the centre line and rises onto his right toes, with flexed knees. She matches the man's turn, rises onto her left toes, knees flexed.

● The man moves back onto his left foot and the woman forward, right foot outside the man's right side.

ep five, quick ◄ **step three, quick, step four, slow** ◄ **step two, quick** ◄ **step one, slow** ■

natural with running finish around a corner

Sometimes, the simplest moves are the best. Use the popular running finish to take you comfortably around a corner while maintaining flow and momentum. Here too is a different start but one, the pattern of which is already familiar, the natural turn.

● The man swings his left side forward and lowers, toe-heel, onto his left foot. The woman matches the man's turn to end, backing along the room, lowering her right foot back, toe-heel. Continue into the Basic Quickstep.

● He then sways to the left, rising onto his right toes. She reaches forward along the room with her left toes, and matching the man's turn, rises onto her left toes as she sways to the right.

● The man moves back along the room onto his left foot and the woman moves forward right foot outside the man's right side. He extends his right foot, pointing the toes parallel to the new wall.

II **step seven, slow** ◀ **step six, quick** ◀ **step five, quick**

He completes the turn to end, ıcking along the room and swaying the right. She corresponds by ɔsing her left foot to her right, then wering onto her left foot, completing e turn to end, facing along the room.

● The woman moves back, a slightly smaller step than the man and turns onto her right toes so her right foot ends to the side. Still on the toes, the man closes his right foot to his left then lowers onto his right foot.

● The woman moves back, her left foot matching the man's turn. He swings his left foot forward on the zig towards the wall and continues to turn right, rising onto his toes.

● Having completed the Basic Quickstep or Lockstep, the man is on his left foot and the woman on her right. He walks forward along the zig, right foot outside her right side, starting to turn right.

tep four, slow **step three, quick** **step two, quick** **step one, slow**

basic

tipple chassé

This is one of the more understated and unhurried ways of getting around a corner. Leave a little space to dance into as you approach the corner. The move starts with steps one to three of the already familiar Natural Turn so that's where we pick up the Tipple Chassé.

● The couple is now ready to continue into either the Basic Quickstep or a corner move, ensuring that the man takes the next step with his right foot forward outside the woman's right side.

● Still moving along the room, the man moves forward lowering, toe heel, onto his left foot, and the woman moves back, lowering, toe-heel, onto her right foot.

● Still on the toes, the man crosses his right foot loosely behind his left foot, and the woman crosses her left foot loosely in front of her right foot

step seven, slow

step six, quick

step five, quick

The dancers now prepare to ·mplete the move with a Lockstep. ıe man swings his left foot forward ɔng the room onto the toes while e woman swings her right back ɔng the room onto the toes.

● Turning onto the zig of the new wall, the man steps side and slightly forward onto his right toes, while the woman corresponds by moving side and slightly back onto her left toes.

● He moves side onto his right toes, turning to face along the room, parallel to the new wall. She moves side onto her left toes, turning to match the man. He closes his left foot to right and she closes her right foot to left.

● With feet closed, the man stands on his right foot backing along the room. The woman is on her left foot facing along the room. He moves back, left foot starting to turn to right and she matches, stepping right foot forward.

:ep four, slow ◀ **step three, quick** **step two, quick** **step one, slow** ◀ ■

intermediate

quickstep

open impetus

This unlocks the door to a range of exciting moves. By overturning it, it can be used along the side of a room. This version can be danced at a corner before a long side, giving you space to enjoy the moves that can follow. As an alternative, replace steps one to three with the Hairpin, in which case the woman moves her right foot forward outside the man's right side on step four.

● The woman keeps her head up, and turns it left to right, to end looking along the floor. Her body opens up as she lowers side, small step, toe-heel, onto her right foot so that her right foot is pointing along the zag.

● The woman moves forward past the man onto her left toes and swivels to face the man. After a brief hover, he lowers to the side, small step, toe-heel, onto his left foot, which is pointing along the zig in promenade position.

● Turning on the left heel, the man pulls his right heel strongly back in contact with the floor to close to his left foot, before rising onto his toes. The man ends on the zig of the new wall.

step six, slow **step five, slow**

The man takes a small step back ıto his left foot, turning right. The ɔman walks forward onto her right ɩot, matching the man's turn. Notice e couple's body shape as they move ːo promenade position.

He closes his right foot to left, then lowers onto his right foot, completing the turn to end, backing along the room. She closes her left foot to right, lowers onto her left foot, completing the turn to end, facing along the room.

The man swings his left foot forward on the zig towards the wall, rising onto his toes and swaying right. The woman steps back and turns onto her right toes, so her right foot ends to the side.

The man walks forward along the zig, right foot outside the woman's right side, starting to turn right. The woman moves back with her left foot, matching the man's turn.

step four, slow **step three, quick** **step two, quick** **step one, slow**

passing natural, outside change

Having danced the Open Impetus, you can now accelerate into the Passing Natural and Outside Change, followed by a Wing and Progressive Chassé to Right. This fantastic flight along the room is both spectacular for the spectator and exhilarating for the dancers.

- The couple is now ready to dance through the middle as they travel along the floor into the Wing or the Hairpin from promenade position, but to a count of slow, quick, slow, followed by a Running Finish.

- She keeps her head up and turns it from left to right, to end looking along the floor. Her body opens up as she lowers side, small step, toe-heel, onto her right foot so that her right foot is pointing along the zag.

- The man lowers to the side, small step, toe-heel, onto his left foot, turning a little to promenade position so that his left foot is pointing along the zig.

He walks back along the room, left
ot, and she walks forward, right foot.
e now rises onto his toes as he
eps back with his right foot, starting
turn left. She matches his step with
er left foot, but does not turn.

● He lowers, toe-heel, as he steps back along the room onto his right foot. She lowers, toe-heel, as she steps forward left foot along the room. He sways right, and she, left, but at the end of the step the sway is neutralised.

● He swings his left side and foot forwards and turns across the line of the room, rising onto his left toes and swaying right to end, backing along the room. She steps forward onto her right toes, matching the man's sway.

● Having completed the Open Impetus, the man and woman walk forward and across themselves – man right foot, woman left foot – through the middle and along the room.

step three, quick | step two, quick | step one, slow

wing and chassé

You have already practised this move in the Waltz (see pages 28–29). Now, it's time to hot it up in Quickstep time for a dazzling finale to the three previous moves. This figure can also be used straight after the Open Impetus.

- The man lowers, toe-heel, as he moves onto his right foot. The woman lowers, toe-heel, as she moves onto her left foot. They are now ready to continue into Outside Change or steps five to eight of Basic Quickstep.

- The man closes his left foot to his right, still on his toes, and continues to turn back along the zig. The woman closes her right foot to her left, still on her toes, matching the man's turn.

- Still moving along the room, the man steps side onto the toes of his right foot, turning to back the wall. Th woman moves side onto the toes of her left foot.

As he moves along the room, the an moves forward onto his left foot ıtside the woman's left side and rns slightly to his left. The woman oves back onto her right foot.

● The woman lowers, toe-heel, forward onto her left foot outside the man's left side and moves her head over to her left. They are now ready to continue with the chassé to right.

● She moves her right side and foot forward onto her toes around the man. Still on his right foot, the man continues turning to the left until he is on the zag facing towards the centre line of the room.

● Having walked through the middle, the couple start to turn left. He stays on his right foot in the centre of the turn, and draws his left foot to his right without weight, guiding the woman around him.

tep four, slow **step three, quick** ◀ **step two, quick** **step one, slow** ◀

natural turn with hesitation

This is similar to the Hesitation Change in Waltz (see pp50–51) but is danced along the side of the room. Step six is modified to provide an elegant entry into the Chassé Reverse Turn. Alternatively, it can be followed by the Chassé element of the Wing and Chassé, with step four being taken in line with your partner.

● The woman matches the man's turn as she dances side on to her left foot. Then the man slides his left foot to his right, and the woman slides her right foot to her left. There is no transfer of weight for either.

● As his right foot slides round, the man swivels on his left foot to end facing along the zag, towards the centre line of the room, then transfers his weight to his right foot.

● The man draws his right foot back heel in contact with the floor, and slides it around so it ends next to his left foot, feet slightly apart.

|| step six, slow ◂ step five, slow ◂ step four, slow

The woman corresponds by closing
›r left foot to her right, lowering
ıto her left foot, and completing the
›rn to end facing along the room. He
›en steps back with his left foot and
e steps forward with her right.

● The woman steps back and turns onto her toes so her right foot ends to the side. Still on his toes, the man closes his right foot to his left, lowers onto his right foot, and completes the turn so he is backing along the room.

● The man swings his left foot forward on the zig towards the wall. As his weight moves onto his left foot, he rises onto his toes, while his body sways to the right.

● From standing on his left foot on the zig, the man walks forward, right foot outside the woman's right side, and turning right. From standing on her right, the woman moves back, her left foot matching the man's turn.

step three, quick **step two, quick** ◀ **step one, slow** ◀ ■

chassé reverse turn

This is not too difficult a combination of two basic moves and one that provides a pleasant change by turning in the opposite direction to normal. Care should be taken as you move away from the wall and into the flow of floor traffic, now approaching from the man's left.

● He moves side along the room, lowering, toe heel, onto his left foot, facing along the zig. She lowers, toe-heel, onto her right foot. They can now repeat the Basic Quickstep, or any natural move, turning to the right.

● Still on his toes, the man closes his right foot to his left, and continues to turn onto the zig. The woman closes her left foot to her right, and matches the man's turn.

● The man moves side along the room onto the toes of his left foot, turning towards the wall. The woman corresponds by moving side onto the toes of her right foot, matching the man's turn.

II ◄ step seven, slow ◄ step six, quick ◄ step five, quick

The man walks back, right foot
ɔng the zag, turning left, while the
ɔman walks forwards, left foot
atching the man's turn.

He closes his left foot to his right, then lowers onto his left foot, completing the turn to end backing along the room. She closes her right foot to her left, lowering onto her right foot to end facing the room.

The woman walks back onto her right foot. He then swings his right foot forwards, rising onto his toes and swaying to the left. She steps back and turns on her left toes, so her left ends to the side.

The man starts facing along the zig towards the centre line of the room, standing on his left foot. The woman is facing the man, standing on her right foot. He walks forward onto his left foot along the zag, curving left.

ɛp four, slow **step three, quick** **step two, quick** **step one, slow**

quick open reverse turn

This is one of the most exciting moves in Quickstep. It starts with a gradual and controlled build up of speed that just explodes at the high point of the turn to almost blow you off your feet! The best place to begin this move is after a Natural Spin Turn, so you are starting to move along the side of the room.

● The man lowers toe-heel, back onto his left foot, and the woman forward onto her right foot outside the man's right side. The couple now continues into the Basic Quickstep, starting with step five.

● Continuing to turn left, the man swings his right side forward past the woman and onto his right toes, swaying left. The woman swings onto her left toes as she takes a smaller step to the side, swaying to the right.

● Still flexed at the knee, the man drives forwards, left foot in line with the woman, and continues to turn le
The woman moves back with her right foot.

step eight, quick ◀ **step seven, quick** ◀ **step six, slow**

The man now flexes through the ee as he drives forward, right foot tside the woman's right side, turning face along the zag. The woman rresponds, walking back across and derneath her body as she turns.

● The man lowers toe-heel, and moves side and forwards along the zag, towards the centre line of the room. The woman lowers toe-heel and moves side and back.

● The man moves side onto his left toes, continuing to turn left. The woman matches the turn as she moves onto her right toes. He then closes his right foot to his left, and she closes her left foot to her right.

● Having completed the Natural Spin Turn, the man is back on his left foot, and the woman is forward on her right. He then moves back on his right foot, turning left. She walks forwards onto her left foot, matching his turn.

woodpecker variation and explosion 1

quickstep

A fantasy of fireworks is afoot culminating in the Explosion while the Woodpecker provides an excellent entry to this exciting combination favoured in various combinations by competitors and experienced dancers.

● Still in promenade position, the man hops in place on his left foot and points his right foot behind along the line but without transferring any weight. The woman corresponds with her left foot.

● Still in promenade position, the man hops in place on his left foot and points his right foot forward through the middle and along the line but without transferring any weight. The woman corresponds with her left foot.

● Still in promenade position, the man closes his right foot to his left foot and the woman her left foot to her right. Still in promenade position, the man and woman move along the room: man, left foot, woman, right foot.

● The man continues onto his left foot, the woman onto her right foot Steps 3 and 4 are syncopated, that is the beat is split quick : &, so that both steps are taken in the same beat.

step eight, quick ◀ step seven, quick ◀ step six, quick step five, quick

The woman is on her left. It is portant to maintain the speed of avel and not to lift off the floor ring this hop. Still in promenade osition, the man and woman move ong the room.

● In this case steps 1 and 2 are taken within the same two beats of music so the Slow count is cut short. Flexing the knees and dancing down in to the floor, the dancers hop along the floor, the man still on the right foot

● The man and woman accelerate forward and across themselves, 'through the middle' and along the room: man right foot, woman left foot. An '&' count is twice as fast as an Quick count.

● Having danced the Open Impetus, the man is standing on his left foot and the woman on her right in promenade position, ready to move along the room.

ep four, &

step three, quick

step two, &

step one, slow

woodpecker variation and explosion 2

The move should be measured so that the climax – the Explosion – occurs at a corner. Of course, you should always take care to avoid kicking other dancers.

● She dances the normal opposite. They resume position as on step 14, turning a little to right, ready to dance along the new wall and continue with a back lock and running finish, starting with step 2 of that move.

step fifteen, quick

● The woman corresponds and taps with her left foot. The Explosion – he now rises abruptly onto his left toes, turning to look back. He sways strongly to right and kicks, left foot, pointed toes, back along the floor.

step fourteen, slow

● He lowers, toe-heel, onto his left footwhile she corresponds with her right foot. The man then relaxes down through the knee, swaying left. He crosses the toes of his right foot behind his left foot to tap the floor.

step thirteen, &

● They move forward and across themselves, 'through the middle' and along the room: man right foot, woman left foot. Still in promenade position, he moves along the room and drops gently.

She corresponds with the normal pposite. Still in promenade position, e man moves along the room and ops gently. He lowers, toe-heel, on his left foot while she corresponds th her right foot.

● Still in promenade position, the man lifts on to the toes of his left foot and drops gently, toe-heel, in place onto his right foot. At the same time, he extends his left foot to point, without weight, along the room.

● Still in promenade position, the man lifts onto the toes of his left foot and then relaxes through the knee to create a bounce action. He taps a second time with his right foot. The woman corresponds with her left foot.

● Still in promenade position, he lifts onto his left toes, relaxing through the knee to create a bounce action while crossing his right toes behind his left foot to tap the floor. She corresponds and taps with her left foot.

ep twelve, slow ◀ **step eleven, quick** ◀ **step ten, quick** ◀ **step nine, quick** ◀ ■

step, hop, slide, scoop and charleston

Originally the Quickstep was called the Quick Time Foxtrot & Charleston before its name was shortened. In this combination, the exuberance of the Roaring Twenties is evoked in a showpiece climax to a powerful and impressive figure, popular with competitors and advanced dancers.

● He points back, right foot, she forward, left foot, swivelling as before. The couple can now exit the move with any other move, starting with the man, moving forward, right foot outside the woman's right side.

● The man points his left foot forward and the woman her right foot back. The man moves back onto his left foot and the woman forward onto her right foot outside the man's right side, swivelling as before.

● The woman corresponds with the opposite foot. The man steps forward, right foot, outside the woman's right side, swivelling the toes outwards. The woman steps backwards, left foot, swivelling the toes outwards.

● The Charleston starts as the man lifts his right leg parallel to the floor, knees together, and swivels his left toes inwards. There is a little bounce action through the knee of the standing leg.

II **step eight, slow** ◀ **step seven, slow** **step six, slow** **step five, &** **step four, slow**

The man rises onto the his left
›es. He sways to right in 'the scoop'.
ıe corresponds with the normal
ɔposite, turning towards him to
ːsume a normal close position while
ɛr head reverts to her left.

● They must maintain speed of travel and not lift off the floor. Flexing well down through the knees to extend their reach, the man takes a long step along the room onto his left foot and the woman onto her right.

● In this case steps 1 and 2 are taken within the same two beats of music so the Slow count is cut short. Dancing down in to the floor, they hop along the floor, the man still on the right foot, and the woman her left.

● From promenade position, they accelerate forward and across themselves, 'through the middle' and along the room: man right foot, woman left foot.

◄ **step three, slow** **step two, &** **step one, slow** ◄

slow foxtrot

the feather finish and three step

slow foxtrot

The graceful and understated elegance of the Slow Foxtrot is that to which all Ballroom dancers aspire. However, unlike the other dances in this book, the Slow Foxtrot does not have a single basic repeatable step pattern. This means that we have to link the Feather Finish, Three Step and Impetus Turn together.

● The man walks forward along the zig lowering, toe-heel, onto his left foot, still swaying to left. The woman walks back, right foot, swaying to right. Now they can complete the Basic Slow Foxtrot group by dancing into the Impetus Turn.

● The man walks forward, right foot, along the zig and rises onto his toes, swaying to left. The woman walks back, left foot, releasing the toe of the front heel, swaying to right. The woman does not go onto her toes.

● The dancers are now ready to dance the Three Step. The man walks forward, left foot, in line with the woman along the zig while the woma walks back, right foot.

II step six, quick ◀ **step five, quick** ◀ **step four,**

Maintaining the same sway, the man ›wers, toe-heel, as he moves right ›t forward, outside the woman's ›ht side along the zig. The woman ›lks back underneath her body onto ›r left foot.

● The woman sways left as she moves side along the zag onto her right foot but, though she feels the rise through her body, does not allow her heels to leave the floor at the end of the step.

● The woman corresponds and moves forwards, a short step, onto her left foot. The man sways to right as he reaches side along the zag, rising onto the toes of his left foot.

● Start on a zig in the normal Ballroom hold, feet together. Prepare to start moving by rising onto the toes. The man lowers through the standing leg as he moves back, a short step onto the right foot.

›ep three, quick **step two, quick** ◀ **step one, slow** ◀ ■

impetus turn

This move, when dovetailed with the Feather Finish and Three Step, allows you to dance a repeatable basic pattern of Slow Foxtrot continuously. It is also useful in other combinations of Slow Foxtrot moves. By reducing by a quarter the amount of turn over the last three steps, it is the ideal at a corner.

● The man steps back, lowering, toe-heel, onto his left foot while the woman steps forward, lowering toe-heel, onto her right foot. The couple is now ready to continue into the Feather Finish and Three Step.

● At the end of this manoeuvre he rises onto the toes as he completes the turn to end facing along the zig. She moves forward onto her left toes, turning to right and touching her right foot to her left in a 'brush'.

● The man pivots on the heel of the left foot, swaying to right and turning to right, while drawing the heel of his right foot back, in contact with the floor, to close to his left foot.

● The man moves back onto his left foot and the woman forward onto he[r] right foot, both starting to turn right.

step four, slow

At the end of this manoeuvre she es onto the toes. The man steps ck along the room, lowering, toe el, onto his right foot. The woman oves forward, lowering, toe heel, ıto her left foot.

step three, quick

● The woman pivots on the heel of the left foot, swaying to left and turning to right, to end facing along the room, while drawing the heel of her right foot back, in contact with the floor, to close to her left foot.

step two, quick

● The woman corresponds by moving back with the left foot. The man swings his left foot forward and moves onto the toes of his left foot, swaying to right as he turns right to end backing along the room.

step one, slow

● Continue from the last step of the Feather Finish and Three Step. The man is on the zig, standing on his left foot and the woman her right. The man walks forward, right foot, along the zig, starting to turn right.

reverse turn

slow foxtrot

The Feather Finish, Three Step and Impetus Turn make up a short, repeatable group of moves. This group can be extended further, into more internationally standard grouping with the addition of one figure between the Feather Finish and the Three Step – the Reverse Turn.

● She walks back underneath her body onto her left foot. They are now ready to dance The Three Step.

● Maintaining the same sway, he lowers toe-heel, as he moves right foot forward outside her right side along the zig.

● He lowers through the standing leg as he moves back a short step onto the right foot. She moves forwards, a short step onto her left foot.

● He steps back along the room, lowering toe-heel, onto his left foot. She moves forward, lowering toe-hee onto her right foot.

step six, quick ◀ step five, quick ◀ step four, slow ◀

She ends facing along the room, ...ile drawing the heel of her left foot ...ck in contact with the floor to close ...her right foot. At the end if this ...anoeuvre, she rises onto her toes.

● He swings his right foot forward and moves onto the toes of his right foot, swaying to left as he turns left to end, backing along the room. She pivots on the heel of her right foot, swaying to right and turning to left.

● The woman is facing the man and back on her left foot. He walks forward, left foot in line with her, along the zag towards the centre line of the room, starting to turn left. She moves back with the left foot.

● Dance the Feather Finish. The man is now facing along the zag towards the centre line of the room, and is foward on his right foot outside the woman's right side.

step three, quick ◀ **step two, quick** ◀ **step one, slow** ◀ ■

reverse wave

The Reverse Wave depicts, as the name suggests, the rise and fall of a gently undulating wave. It is a great figure to dance and it can be a substitute for the Three Step after the Feather Finish and before the Impetus Turn to give additional length to the combination.

● He ends backing along the room, by stepping back, lowering, toe-heel, onto his right foot without allowing the heel of his left foot to lower. She moves forward again, lowering toe-heel onto her left foot.

● He walks back onto his left toes, swaying to right. The woman walks forward, right foot, rising from the heel onto the toes, swaying to left. The man completes his curve.

● The man walks back again, right foot, and the woman walks forward, left foot. The couple are now starting to dance along a gentle curve that will end with the man backing along the room by step six.

● At the end of this manoeuvre she rises onto her toes. The man steps back along the zig, lowering, toe-heel onto his left foot. The woman moves forward, lowering, toe-heel, onto her right foot.

step six, quick ◄ step five, quick ◄ step four, slow

The woman pivots on the heel of
e right foot, swaying to right and
ning to left to end facing along the
, while drawing the heel of her left
ot back in contact with the floor to
se to her right foot.

step three, quick

● The man swings his right foot forward and moves onto the toes of his right foot, swaying to left as he turns right to end, backing along the zig.

step two, quick

● The man walks forward, left foot in line with the woman, along the zig, starting to turn left. The woman corresponds by moving back with the right foot.

● Begin having danced steps 1–3 of the Feather Finish or a complete Reverse Turn. The man is forward right foot outside the woman's right side, and the woman is back on her left foot.

step one, slow

slow foxtrot

open impetus turn

The last three steps of the Impetus Turn can be modified to end in promenade position and so give the dancers the opportunity to enjoy some of the moves that start in that position as they build their repertoire. By reducing the amount of turn by quarter, this is a great figure to use at a corner too.

● The woman moves along the zag towards the centre line of the room, lowering toe-heel, onto her right foot in promenade position and having moved her head to look along the direction of travel.

● As she does this, she starts to move her head to right into the now familiar promenade position. The man moves along the zag towards the centre line of the room, lowering toe heel, on to his left foot in promenade position.

● He ends facing almost along the room. The woman moves forward onto the toes of her left foot, turning to right and touching her right foot to her left in a 'brush'.

II step six, quick

step five, quick

He turns to right, while drawing the :el of his right foot back, in contact th the floor, to close to his left foot. : the end of this manoeuvre he es onto the toes as he completes e turn.

● The man moves back onto his left foot, and the woman forward onto her right foot, both starting to turn right. The man pivots on the heel of the left foot, swaying to right.

● Dance steps 1–3 of the Impetus Turn (see pages 108–109).

● Begin having danced the Three Step. The man is facing along the zig and is forward on his left foot. The woman corresponds, and is back on her right foot.

:ep four, slow

step three, quick ◀

step two, quick

step one, slow ◀ ■

open telemark to outside swivel

This is one of the most graceful sequences of the Slow Foxtrot. It gives the dancers a great opportunity to display their virtuosity.

● The dancers are now ready to continue into the Weave.

● Although not strictly 'correct', many ladies embellish this move by allowing the left foot to circle out to the side a little during the swivel.

● The woman walks right forward outside the man's right side and swivels to right on the right foot all the way round to end in a promenade position.She is now ready to move along the zag towards the centre line.

● But, at the end of the step, the swa is neutralised.The man takes a short step back along the zig onto his left foot, crossing his right foot. Pivoting or his left foot he turns right, facing the centre line of the room along the zag.

step eight, slow **step seven, slow** **step six, quick** **step five, quick**

The man lowers, toe-heel, as he :ps back along the room onto his :ht foot. The woman lowers, toe-heel, she steps forward left foot along the om. During the step, the man sways right and the woman to left.

● He rises onto the toes of the left foot, swaying to right and ending backing along the zig. The woman continues forward along the zig onto the toes of her right foot, matching the man's sway.

● The man and woman walk forward and across themselves, 'through the middle' and along the zig: man right foot, woman left foot. The man swings his left side, foot strongly forward, turning across the zig.

● Dance the Open Telemark as described in the Waltz Section, underturning it to end ready to move along the zig. The count will be slow, quick, quick.

:ep four, slow **step three, quick** **step two, quick** ◀ **step one, slow** ◀ ■

weave

Having danced the Open Impetus Turn, the dancers are set to enjoy the gentle 'floating' feeling of the Weave. The effect is created while dancing on the toes by relaxing the knees so that they act to soften the impact of each step and maintain that elegance of flow in the movement.

● The man walks forward along the zig, outside the woman's right side, lowering toe-heel, onto his right foot. She walks back underneath her body, along the zig, lowering toe-heel, onto her left foot. They can continue with the Three Step.

● Still turning left, the man points the toes of his left foot towards the wall, transferring his weight onto the toes of his left foot. The woman moves forward onto the toes of her right foot, still turning left to end backing the wall.

● The man steps back along the room onto the toes of his right foot, continuing to turn left. The woman walks forward along the room, in line with the man, onto the toes of her left foot.

II step seven, quick ◄ **step six, quick** ◄ **step fiive, quick**

The man moves back underneath e body onto the toes of his left foot, ontinuing to turn left. The woman alks forward along the room and utside the man's right side onto the es of her right foot.

● She resumes normal hold. Her head resumes its normal position to left. The man moves side onto the toes of his right foot, continuing to turn left to end backing the zig while the woman moves side onto her left toes.

● The man takes a small step forward, along the zag and between the woman's feet, onto the toes of his left foot, starting to turn left. The woman turns left across the man, stepping side onto her right toes.

● The man walks forward and across, along the zag towards the centre line of the room, onto his right foot. The woman corresponds with her left foot.

tep four, quick ◄ step three, quick ◄ step two, quick ◄ step one, slow ◄

hover cross with feather finish 1

The Hover Cross is a classic Foxtrot figure and can be used along the side of the room or, by a little adjustment of the exit position, at a corner. The move provides a pause in the movement without interrupting the flow – a great figure, especially when you get a double helping!

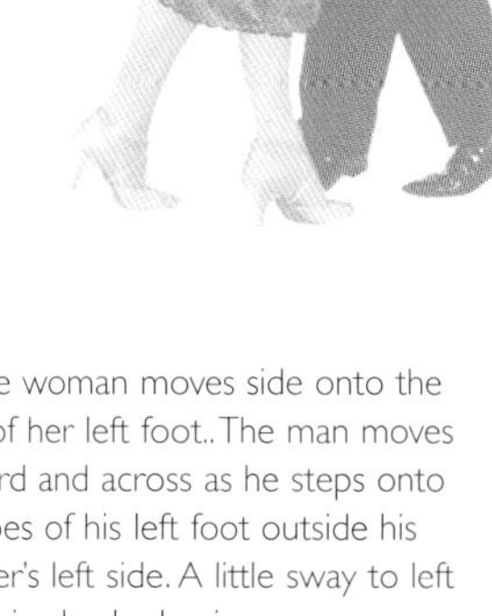

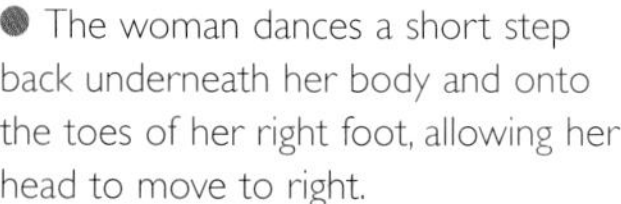

● The woman dances a short step back underneath her body and onto the toes of her right foot, allowing her head to move to right.

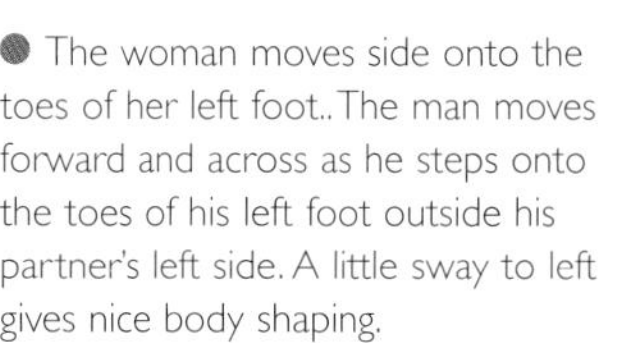

● The woman moves side onto the toes of her left foot.. The man moves forward and across as he steps onto the toes of his left foot outside his partner's left side. A little sway to left gives nice body shaping.

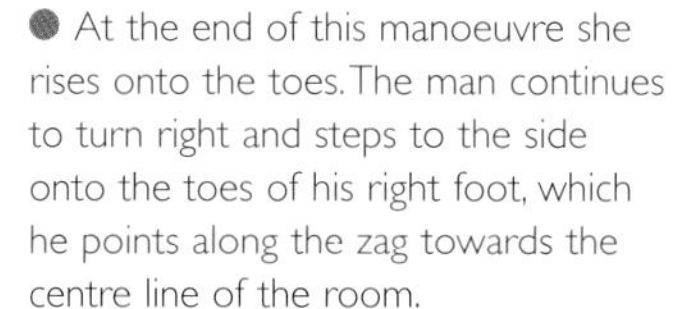

● At the end of this manoeuvre she rises onto the toes. The man continues to turn right and steps to the side onto the toes of his right foot, which he points along the zag towards the centre line of the room.

● The woman pivots on the heel of the left foot, swaying to left and turning to right, to end facing along the room, while drawing the heel of her right foot back, in contact with th floor, to close to her left foot.

II step four, quick ◄ step three, quick ◄

The man swings his left foot
rward and moves onto the toes of
s left foot, swaying to right as he
rns right to end, backing along the
om.

● The man walks forward, right foot, along the zig, starting to turn right. The woman corresponds by moving back with the left foot.

● The man is facing along the zig and is forward on his left foot. The woman corresponds and is back on her right foot.

● Since this can substitute for an Impetus Turn, the starting position is the same. The couple has just completed the Three Step.

hover cross with feather finish 2

Though using the same foot pattern, we will now see how the second Hover Cross gives the dancers an opportunity to change the body shape. This acts as a counter-balance to the shaping in the first, adding an amusing embellishment to an already stylish move. It is this attention to detail that helps define the better dancer.

● The woman moves back onto her left foot, underneath her body, releasing the toes of her right foot from the floor. The couple will now continue into, for example, the Open Telemark or Reverse Turn.

● The man moves forward outside the woman's right side facing along the zag, lowering toe-heel, onto his right foot.

● The woman corresponds by moving along the zag but lowering, toe-heel, onto her right foot.

The man now moves onto the toes his left foot along the zag towards e centre line of the room.

● The man leaves his feet in place and transfers his weight again onto his right foot and the woman corresponds by transferring her weight onto her left foot.

● The man transfers his weight onto his left foot, this time swaying a little to right and looking over the woman's left shoulder. The woman transfers her weight to her right foot and moves her head over to left.

● The man leaves his feet in place and transfers his weight again onto his right foot and the woman corresponds by transferring her weight onto her left foot.

same foot lunge

slow foxtrot

The Same Foot Lunge is a 'picture figure', so called because it is the type of move that shows off the line.

● The woman walks forward onto her left foot and, turning to face the man, lifts onto the toes of her left foot. The couple is now ready to continue into the Outside Swivel for a really classy ending to a classic figure.

● The man, his left leg extended to the side, now transfers his weight onto his left foot, turning the woman towards him. Once on his left foot, he turns left to back along the zig as he rises onto his toes. This feels like a scooping action.

● The woman points her right foot back along the room, transferring her weight onto that foot, keeping her knees together to ensure a straight front leg, and thus a good leg line.

● The man flexes his left knee and extends his right foot to the side and points the toes. He transfers his weigh sideways onto his right foot, looking at his partner.

The woman steps forward, right foot ıtside the man's right side, then ʋivels on her right foot, bringing her et together to face back along the ›om. She then transfers her weight to ɜr left foot when the feet close.

● The man walks backwards along the room onto his left foot and pulls his right foot to close but without weight. As he does this he turns right to face the centre line of the room.

● The woman corresponds and is back on her right foot. Dance the Natural Hairpin as described in the Quickstep, pages 76–77, noting that in Slow Foxtrot, Step 1 will be taken in line with the partner.

● Since this can substitute for an Impetus Turn, the starting position is the same. The couple has just completed the Three Step. The man is facing along the zig and is forward on his left foot.

index

Q

R

S

T

W

Z